T0328469

Cambridge Elements ≡

Elements in Public and Nonprofit Administration
edited by
Andrew Whitford
University of Georgia
Robert Christensen
Brigham Young University

TRUST IN GOVERNMENT AGENCIES IN THE TIME OF COVID-19

Scott E. Robinson
University of Oklahoma

Kuhika Gupta
University of Oklahoma

Joseph Ripberger
University of Oklahoma

Jennifer A. Ross
University of Oklahoma

Andrew Fox
University of Oklahoma

Hank Jenkins-Smith
University of Oklahoma

Carol Silva
University of Oklahoma

CAMBRIDGE
UNIVERSITY PRESS

University Printing House, Cambridge CB2 8BS, United Kingdom

One Liberty Plaza, 20th Floor, New York, NY 10006, USA

477 Williamstown Road, Port Melbourne, VIC 3207, Australia

314–321, 3rd Floor, Plot 3, Splendor Forum, Jasola District Centre,
New Delhi – 110025, India

103 Penang Road, #05–06/07, Visioncrest Commercial, Singapore 238467

Cambridge University Press is part of the University of Cambridge.

It furthers the University's mission by disseminating knowledge in the pursuit of education, learning, and research at the highest international levels of excellence.

www.cambridge.org
Information on this title: www.cambridge.org/9781108959551
DOI: 10.1017/9781108961400

First published 2021

A catalogue record for this publication is available from the British Library.

ISBN 978-1-108-95955-1 Paperback
ISSN 2515-4303 (online)
ISSN 2515-429X (print)

Trust in Government Agencies in the Time of COVID-19

Elements in Public and Nonprofit Administration

DOI: 10.1017/9781108961400
First published online: October 2021

Scott E. Robinson
University of Oklahoma
Kuhika Gupta
University of Oklahoma
Joseph Ripberger
University of Oklahoma
Jennifer A. Ross
University of Oklahoma
Andrew Fox
University of Oklahoma
Hank Jenkins-Smith
University of Oklahoma
Carol Silva
University of Oklahoma

Author for correspondence: Scott E. Robinson, Robinson.bellmon@gmail.com

Abstract: As the United States faced its lowest levels of reported trust in government, the COVID-19 crisis revealed the essential service that various federal agencies provide as sources of information. This Element explores variations in trust across various levels of government and government agencies based on a nationally representative survey Started in March 2020. First, it examines trust in agencies including the Department of Health and Human Services, state health departments, and local health care providers. This includes variation across key characteristics including party identification, age, and race. Second, the Element explores the evolution of trust in health-related organizations throughout 2020 as the pandemic continued. The Element concludes with a discussion of the implications for agency-specific assessments of trust and their importance as we address historically low levels of trust in government. This title is also available as Open Access on Cambridge Core.

Keywords: emergency management, public health, COVID-19, trust in government, survey methodology

ISBNs: 9781108959551 (PB), 9781108961400 (OC)
ISSNs: 2515-4303 (online), 2515-429X (print)

Contents

1 Introduction: A Crisis in Trust and Trust in a Crisis

In the spring of 2020, people across the world found their lives disrupted by the prospect of COVID-19. In a matter of days, people experienced massive changes to aspects of their lives that they had taken for granted. Bars closed while restaurants moved to delivery and pick-up models. In some places, the ability to travel was greatly restricted, either by direct limitations or by consequence of many businesses simply being closed. At this time, people clamored for information. What is the risk one faces with COVID-19,[1] and how does it vary across people with different health conditions? What steps are effective at reducing the probability of infection? Where can one turn for reliable information on risks and the sorts of actions we can take to reduce the risks?

At the heart of these questions was an underlying concern about the availability of credible information. The COVID-19 crisis struck in a time when the media environment for sharing information has become fragmented and politicized. Conservatives complain about the "lamestream media" while liberals criticize the reliance of conservatives on "Faux News." The fragmentation extends to social media platforms where information, and misinformation, is easy to share and separating reliable information from noise is challenging. Consider this example (from May 16, 2020). Various locations were beginning to reduce restrictions on travel and commerce. Other locations are still either asking or demanding that people wear cloth masks when in stores. So one might reasonably want to know how well a cloth mask reduces risk of infection (for oneself or for others). It turns out that the answer to this question is tricky. A simple Google search for "are cloth masks effective" turns up 85.5 million hits.[2] The list starts with a page from the US Centers for Disease Control and Prevention (US CDC) on their recommendations for wearing cloth masks – including instructions on what constitutes a minimally protective mask, how to differentiate these masks from N95 and surgical masks, and how (and how not) to clean or make cloth masks. The next couple of links take one to similar

---

[1] There is some confusion over the terminology related to COVID-19. Properly speaking, the viral agent is called SARS-COV-2 and is a member of the class of coronaviruses. COVID-19 is the disease (early on, a syndrome) that is caused by SARS-COV-2. For ease of reading, we will largely use the term COVID-19 to cover the disease and its agent, as this has become the most common term used by the general public to refer to both. We will only distinguish SARS-COV-2 when we need to emphasize the viral agent itself.

[2] The proceeding discussion relating to the specifics of Google search results reflects the author's experience searching for information on the efficacy of masks. The specific figures are reflective of his experience on May 16, 2020, but will not be indicative of any later search or a search by a different person. Every Google or YouTube search is conditional on the account that searches, the history of the account, the location of the search, and contemporaneous searches – even the clicking activities of other people using similar search terms

information from the Mayo and Cleveland Clinics. From there, the information becomes more divided. The fourth link is to an article from Medical News Today (a popular website for general health information) questioning the usefulness of cloth masks compared to more specialized masks. After the fourth link, Google breaks in with a special set of "common questions." The next set of links connect to discussions of the mixed evidence on the usefulness of masks (associated with credible places, such as the University of Minnesota and the popular website LiveScience).

This Youtube search in May 2020 produced results that start with a link to the popular fact-checking site Snopes and its report that a popular captioned image appealing for people to wear masks based on their ability to protect others from transmission of the virus is "mostly false." Of course, reading deeper into the Snopes report indicates that their evaluation is based on the lack of citations to back up the risk percentages on the popular graphic. The Snopes report does not indicate that cloth masks are ineffective – only that a specific popular graphic did not include evidence for its own statements. However, it would not be hard to mistake the criticism of the specific chart with a more general conclusion that cloth masks are demonstrably ineffective. The videos that follow include a review of a prominent research article supporting the effectiveness of surgical masks, a video from the World Health Organization (WHO) (from early February 2020) arguing that one should only wear masks in limited situations due to a shortage of surgical masks at the time, and a video from a person calling himself the "Genius Asian" who compares the effectiveness of a surgical mask and a sock in their ability to filter flour using a vacuum cleaner.

This is the challenge that an interested person faces trying to find answers to simple but important questions about the effectiveness of proposed protective actions. Information on the effectiveness of masks is fragmented and hard to follow. There are debates between reputable sources over the exact level of effectiveness – a debate for which the conclusion is still very much unresolved. There is old information (like the February WHO video, from a time when wearing masks was actively discouraged to prevent shortages in hospitals) and information from sorces of unknown credibility such as the "Genius Asian." Even someone who has a great deal of training in understanding scientific articles (particularly the statistics underlying them) and has attempted to keep up with latest news related to COVID-19 cannot find a clear and compelling answer to a question as simple as how much wearing a cloth mask reduces the risk of infection.

What does one do in such circumstances? This is not an unusual situation. Many questions central to our daily lives depend on staggeringly complicated processes. Is our food safe from contamination? Will a new medicine help us with a health problem? Is our personal information safe when we purchase something online? It is impossible for each of us to know the answer to such questions. In fact, any valid answer is unlikely to take the form of "yes" or "no." Yet we have to act in our world based on our belief in the safety of our food supply, the effectiveness of medicines, the adequacy of data protection, and so many other issues.

What we do is trust. We trust in others to tell us whether our food is safe, to prevent contamination, and to inform us if there is a break in this safety. We trust in our medical professionals to weigh risks and prescribe us medicine that will address our health problems without creating worse side effects. We expect that regulatory regimes and technological advancement will ensure the safety of our private information. Very few of us can explain how these safety systems operate. There may be no one who can rightly consider themself an expert in even these three domains. Instead, we all have to trust in the expertise and authority of others. But what happens, then, if that trust is tested? That is the core subject of this Element.

This Element is grounded in a series of surveys conducted during a period of great uncertainty. As word of the COVID-19 crisis began to emerge in late January and early February of 2020, the authors met to discuss the possibility of a national survey of residents of the United States to assess how people were understanding the risks associated with the disease. By March, we had a survey in the field that included questions about individual risk perceptions, the willingness to take certain precautions to prevent the spread of the virus, and trust in a range of relevant organizations. We wanted to know what people feared, who they trusted, and what they were willing to do to protect themselves. March was, in the United States in particular, an important transition point in the fight against the pandemic. It was on March 12 that the WHO declared COVID-19 to be a pandemic. About this time, US states and cities began various efforts to combat the spread of the disease. The survey results reported here come from this uncertain time period when people did not know much about the risks and sought answers, with some tracking of how reported trust evolved through the pandemic (up to November 2020).

The Element explores the variations in reported trust in various agencies relevant to the COVID-19 response in US cities and states, as well as abroad. This exploration intends to drill down into the data to better understand who trusts different organizations and how trust varies across various social groups including political parties and age groups. The results also include a track of the changes in trust over the summer and fall of 2020 in the United States as pandemic response became politicized – often thought to be captured in the polarization politically exaggerated by the presidential election in November

2020. Together, the results provide some evidence for the variety of assessments the public has for agencies providing key health information during the pandemic – as well as their shared destiny.

1.1 The Recent History of Trust in Government in the United States

Our investigation begins with a brief review of how the United States found itself in the position of distrust in official agencies. Pollsters have asked questions related to trust in government in US-based surveys for decades. The Pew Trust has summarized decades of these polls (2019). Figure 1 illustrates the trend in polls from the late 1950s to 2019.

Infrequent polling on the topic began in the late 1950s in the tail of what some see as a postwar consensus period of limited partisan conflict and high levels of participation in major social institutions. Government was relatively popular in this period as it was seen by some as having both pulled the United States out of the Great Depression and overseen a successful end to World War II. The emerging conflict with the Soviet Union served more to rally the US public together in support of its government than to fuel divides along partisan lines. The result was an era reporting the highest levels of trust in the US government seen in the seventy-year period over which we have reliable polling data.

This early period preceded the modern pattern of extensive polling of the US public. As a result, there are fewer data points with which to explore this time. The period from the late 1950s through the mid-1970s is charted based on individual polls and never more than one a year. The period

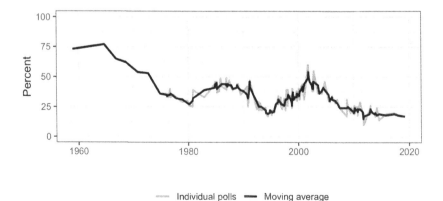

Figure 1 A time series of "trust in government" poll averages from the late 1950s through 2019

begins with averages of reported trust in the range of 75 percent at its peak (in the early 1960s) and beginning a period of decline that continues through the start of the 1980s. It is interesting to note that the decline preceded the Watergate scandals of the early to mid-1970s. The Watergate scandals certainly did not reverse the trend of declining trust, but it also did not seem to accelerate this decline. One clear consequence from the figure was a dramatic increase in the polling on trust in government in the mid-1970s. We start to see multiple polls in a given year. At this point in Figure 1, the faded grey line indicates individual polls with the darker line continuing to report the moving annual average. There is variation around the moving average, but it provides a useful track of the central tendency of the individual polls.

The long downward trend in trust began to reverse in the early 1980s. This era was known for the generally optimistic presidential campaigns for President Ronald Reagan. His 1980 campaign slogans included the phrase "Let's Make American Great Again," while his 1984 reelection slogans included the phrase "It's Morning in America Again." These slogans were taken by many as a call for a change in direction (following stagflation and the oil crisis of the late 1970s under the Carter Administration), while also pointing toward great opportunities in the future. Of course, this increased optimism was not a return to the generally pro-government attitudes of the postwar consensus period. Reagan attacked the government as the source of, rather than solution to, the public's problems. Famously, in 1986, while president, Reagan said during one of his press conferences that "the nine most terrifying words in the English language are 'I'm from the government and I'm here to help.'"[3]

This period was by no means a high mark for the support for large government programs. It was, however, a period in which trust in government grew over its late-1970s lows. The growth in trust, though, maxed out below 50 percent before a new period of decline began in the mid- to late 1980s. The Reagan Administration became mired in scandals like the Iran-Contra affair that cast a shadow over the (successful) election campaign of Bush, then vice president, in 1988. There was a brief spike in trust around the time of the Gulf War in 1990–1991 but it proved short-lived. The downward trajectory continued as a recession hit the United States in 1990. This recession proved to be a strong influence on the 1992 election season with President Clinton defeating President Bush's reelection attempt. The decline in trust continued through the early

---

[3] Presidential news conference, August 12, 1986; see www.reaganfoundation.org/ronald-reagan/reagan-quotes-speeches/news-conference-1/.

1990s and was not reversed until the US economy had pulled well away from the recession of the same time period.

A trend of increasing trust began in the mid-1990s (not immediately following the election of President Clinton to his first term in the 1992 election) and continued though 2001. This period was not without its scandals, and we see short-term drops in trust – possibly related to the major scandals of the late 1990s including the Monica Lewinsky affair and subsequent impeachment of President Clinton. Furthermore, the Clinton Administration contributed to the sense that government agencies were often wasteful with their effort to "reinvent government." The attacks on government in this time period were consistently parts of presidential administrations from the Carter Administration forward (Arnold, 1998). This period of rising trust is punctuated with a dramatic increase in reported trust that coincides with the 9/11 terrorist attacks on the United States. It is important to note, however, that this period of increasing trust reached its maximum at reported survey averages of just above 50 percent. This peak is well below the early (albeit scantily recorded) eras of trust at or above 75 percent.

The surge in support following the 9/11 attacks was followed by a long-term downward trajectory in trust that continues, albeit with some leveling out, through 2019. This downward trajectory continued through the George W. Bush (43) Administration. Around the time of the 2008 election, won by Barack Obama, we see a leveling out of the downward trend. There were no signs of anything more than a temporary increase in trust from the Obama Administration, through the 2016 election, and through the first three years of the Trump Administration. What had been a series of cycles of increasing and decreasing trust gave way to a steadily low level of trust. It is interesting to note that the cycles had lasted about fifteen years between the 1970s through about 2010. However, there was no turn into a new cycle of increased trust around 2010 as one might expect based on the previous two cycles. Instead, this period returned a flat, low level of trust – as if we were simply missing an anticipated cycle of increased trust (a positive cycle expected from about 2010 to about 2018 with an expected turn negative around 2018). Instead of a cycle of increasing (and eventually decreasing) trust, the late 2010s have been characterized by deep suspicion of government – including charges by the governing party of resistance by a "deep state."

This quick review of the recent history is quite simplistic. Two forms of simplification stand out most. First, the polls report "trust in government" as if people have uniform assessments of all of government. This simplification matches some of the rhetoric described earlier related to attacks on the reputation of government. Reagan had attacked the people "from the government" (generally), Clinton called for a "reinvention of government" (generally), and the recent discussion of the "deep state" suggests a massive conspiracy that crosses traditional agency boundaries and might as well be referring to all government agencies. These rhetorical attacks on government (in times of increasing and decreasing trust) have long considered all government agencies to be of a type – generally a wasteful or rogue type.

Through this period, there is less information on the perception of specific agencies than there is a summary of government as a whole. Infrequent polls by Pew have revealed considerable variation in the perceived effectiveness of US federal agencies. Taking the most recent of these polls in 2019, Pew reported that respondents had highly favorable ratings of the US Postal Service and the US Centers for Disease Control and Prevention (US CDC) (2019). The list of low-rated agencies is familiar to those who follow criticism of government in this time period. Among the lowest are the Department of Education, the Internal Revenue Service, the Environmental Protection Agency, and the Department of Veterans Affairs. Relatively new in this time period is a low level of favorability for the Department of Justice – embroiled in the politics of criminal investigations of the then current Trump Administration and of the campaign of its 2016 opponent, Hillary Clinton.

The second simplification is to aggregate survey responses to a general average. The general average conceals a great deal of variation within every pool. For every period of low trust, there are some who still report high levels of trust in government. For every period of high trust, there were always skeptics. The averages conceal this variation, but the range of the variations indicates the broad variety of perceptions among the respondents. It is the variation that agencies and the government as a whole see in their assessments that inspires hope that they can build or rebuild trust. Pippa Norris argued that there is not a long-term decline in trust but rather a series of multidimensional changes following a "trendless fluctuation" (2001). The notion that the long-term trends conceal variations in trust motivates much of this project.

This leaves us at a point in 2020 where we have settled into an unprecedented period of stability at a low overall level of trust in government. During this period, various government agencies face a novel crisis. Many agencies seek to persuade the public to take self-protective actions ranging from wearing a mask to limiting travel. Other agencies may seek to enforce local rules ranging from occupancy limits on restaurants to beach closures. All of these agencies act within the context of historical low levels of trust. Understanding the context of agencies, actions in this period of low trust is essential to formulating careful strategies for agencies to do their work in the crisis.

1.2 Research Question

How much variation is there in trust in key actors and organizations during their efforts to combat COVID-19? This research question leads in a variety of directions and opens up various avenues for investigation. This book is intended to provide some initial insight into how the trust in specific agencies varies across agencies operating at the local, state, and federal levels and how trust evolved through the pandemic. Do people trust their local agencies more than they do more distant federal agencies? It was the federal agencies, after all, that served as the targets for most attacks on government from the Reagan through Clinton administrations to the contemporary rhetoric of the "deep state." If there is a premium of trust at the local level, this suggests the possibility that a robust local-based strategy for crisis response will face fewer problems related to trust.

The starting point for this investigation is in building a theory of trust in public health actors and organizations. The next section takes up this challenge and reviews relevant literature to build a specific set of expectations for trust in public health agencies and the linkage between this trust and reported willingness to take personal protective actions.

2 A Theory of Trust in Agencies

As the COVID-19 crisis raged across the world, people clamored for information that would help them better understand how to reduce the risks. People wondered whether food preparation would be safe and whether they could order food for delivery. If a sick employee is involved in the preparation of a meal, does that mean that the virus would likely be spread to the people eating the food? Would wearing a mask in public greatly reduce the risk of contracting the virus from others? Does it matter if the mask is a surgical-grade mask, or can a simple cloth covering or bandanna suffice? Any search for information quickly turned up vague or conflicting information. People had to decide which sources of information they trust to guide their behavior when their life may be at stake.

Dr. Jay Baruch, writing in Statnews, provides a poignant account of the frustration and its relation to trust. Dr. Baruch is an associate professor of emergency medicine and director of the medical humanities and bioethics concentration at Brown University. In late March, Dr. Baruch was visiting his emergency department frequently and adjusting to changing protocols for protective equipment. Dr. Baruch writes:

> What I can't track or make sense of is the response from leaders who should
> be bastions of guidance and support. One day we're told that providers must

scrupulously don an N95 mask, face shield, portable gown, and gloves. Then the shortage of personal protective equipment somehow alters scientific evidence, and the Centers for Disease Control and Prevention now believes that surgical masks, which fit like a pair of old khakis, should be more than adequate.
And we can reuse the N95 and surgical masks which, after a day or two, take on a mysterious odor.
I know what that smell is now. It's mistrust.[4]

Dr. Baruch's frustration is with the conflicting information coming from "leaders" including a specific reference to the vacillation of the US CDC on the recommendation to wear masks in public (or not). Though an expert in emergency medicine with far more resources than most to seek advice on personal protection, Dr. Baruch found leaders split and their advice unhelpful. The situation is only worse for most people without access to this knowledge and professional advice networks. Most importantly, for our purposes, Dr. Baruch connects the confusion to trust and mistrust. He wants to trust organizations to provide him consistent, accurate, and timely information, but the lack of consistent messaging has eroded his trust.

Dr. Baruch was not alone in his frustrations. Reporting after the initial period (in June 2020), Politico quotes former acting director of the US CDC Richard Besser as stating,

Trust is the critical factor. You develop trust by being transparent, by explaining on a daily basis what you do know, don't know and what you are doing to get more information.[5]

Given the importance of trust, we must understand how trusted key health information providers were at the start of the COVID-19 pandemic and how trust varied across key organizations. The starting point for this investigation must be a clear understanding of the meaning of trust to support a robust measurement strategy. This section will review the literature on trust with special attention to trust in political authorities. Definitions of trust begin with a foundational analogy for interpersonal trust. This analogy was later adapted to the context of trust in political regimes, and, eventually, a literature emerges considering the role of trust in specific administrative organizations. It is this more recent literature on trust in specific administrative agencies that motivates this

---

[4] "Abandoned by U.S. leaders, the only COVID-19 protection I can count on in my emergency department is trust." March 27, 2020. www.statnews.com/2020/03/27/trust-only-covid-19-protection-emergency-room/.
[5] "Why America is scared and confused: Even the experts are getting it wrong." Politico, March 31, 2020. www.politico.com/news/2020/03/31/experts-coronavirus-cdc-158313.

Element's investigation into the dynamics of trust in organizations combating the COVID-19 pandemic.

2.1 Foundations of a Theory of Trust

As we seek to understand the degree to which people trust an administrative agency, the starting point has to be a careful consideration of trust as a concept. Often, trust in government research has left ambiguous the scenario in which a person may or may not report trust in government. It is clear that this trust is an attitude that a person has – rather than a specific behavior. It is supposed that the attitude may be linked to behaviors, but these behaviors are typically left out of the investigations of trust themselves (for an exception, see Scholz and Lubell, 1998). Trust, as an attitude, is seen as an attitude that warrants investigation on its own merits (Uslaner, 2018). Understanding this attitude requires paring away context to reveal the heart of the concept.

At its heart, trust is a relationship. Trust involves two (or more) actors who are connected in some way. It is useful to start with the simplest case – two individuals (X_i and X_j). Trust is a relationship connecting X_i and X_j. Specifically, trust is a relationship in which X_i (the trustor) voluntarily makes themselves vulnerable to the decisions or actions of X_j (the trustee) – usually with the aspiration of an even greater payoff than would be possible without trust. For example, I may trust my neighbor to feed my dog while I am away on vacation. I may do that because, while it creates a vulnerability (if my neighbor fails to feed my dog, my dog will suffer), it allows me to pursue a greater interest (my vacation).

The dominant approach to analyzing this relationship relies on rational choice modeling. For Coleman (1994, 99), the decision to trust reduces to three variables:

1. p_j = chance of receiving the gain (the probability that the trustee (X_j) is trustworthy)
2. L = potential loss (if trustee (X_j) is untrustworthy)
3. G = potential gain (if trustee (X_j) is trustworthy)

A trustor (X_i) will trust a trustee (X_j) if

$$\frac{p_j}{1-p_j} > \frac{L}{G} \tag{1}$$

A situation like the vacation example motivates James Coleman's model of trust (1994). In this model, Coleman argues that the decision to trust implies a balance of three considerations – what is gained by trust (G)? What is made vulnerable by trust (L)? What is the probability that the trustee will violate the trust (p)? The most important implication of this approach is that any statement about trust must include the trustor, the trustee, and the stakes of the trust. Trust is never a matter of whether X_i simply trusts X_j. Trust is always about whether X_i trusts X_j to take a specific action – because it is specific actions that will define G, L, and p.

The most prominent interpretation of this rational choice model is that which Hardin calls the "encapsulated interest" approach (2002). Hardin argues that trust implies that the trustor has decided that it is in the interest of the trustee to act as the trustor wants them to. The interests of the trustor, then, are included within the self-interests of the trustee. Encapsulation may be the product of interest convergence or the part of institutional design that forces an alignment of interests. In this interpretation, it is forward-looking estimation of the interests of the two parties that drives the definition of p.

To this point, the focus has been on the decision of the trustor to trust the trustee. It is important to also reverse the approach and consider what it is about specific trustees that makes them more compelling to potential trustors. In Hardin's language, what is it about a trustee that makes this particular trustee more likely to encapsulate the trustor's interests? This engages the concept of trustworthiness rather than trust (Levi, 1998, 99). Trust-based approaches and trustworthiness-based approaches are entirely compatible but have different foci. One can develop explanations for the trust relationship that include factors related to the trustor (individual characteristics, experiences, and attitudes) as well as the trustee. This is no more problematic than arguing that the probability of a person buying a soft drink depends on consumer characteristics (income, age, etc.) and characteristics of the soft drink itself (calorie content, flavor, etc.). We can consider both trustor predispositions toward a trustee and characteristics of the trustee as part of how one defines p.

It is important to note that there are alternatives to the rational choice approach of Coleman. March and Olsen, for example, discuss trust from an institutional theory perspective that directly rejects the forward-looking calculations of the rational choice model (March and Olsen, 1989). Their institutional approach focuses on the identities and roles of the trustor and the trustee. Rather than looking forward to expected utility and calculating elements like the ratio of $\frac{G}{L}$, the institutional approach focuses on how individuals use habit and history to identify their own role and whether trust is warranted by their role and the role of the trustee. This approach is commonly left implicit.

Finally, one must also consider the nature of the stakes for the delegation implied in the act of trust. This is the least-often-considered element of the core trust model – a point that will become clear through this review.

However, the nature of the risk (the ratio of $\frac{G}{L}$), as perceived by the trustor, is a major component of the decision. This implies that different Gs and Ls will lead to different trust decisions. This stipulation makes it challenging to compare studies of trust that operate within quite different types of risks and relationships (trust related to information on self-protection during a pandemic versus trust related to information on competing brands of soft drinks).

The most fundamental, and purest, case of trust is interpersonal trust – as implied by Coleman's simple model based on individuals i and j. This involves situations where a specific individual decides whether to trust a specific other individual to perform a specific (vulnerability-inducing) task. This dyadic relationship has been expanded to less direct relationships. Instead of referring to a specific relationship between two individuals who know each other, social trust asks about the predisposition of an individual to report trust in others in their community. The social trust approach focuses on the characteristics of the trustor as a baseline for, presumably, many potential trust relationships to other, unnamed individuals – typically without specifying a specific task or vulnerability.

The shift to social trust requires a slight modification of the Coleman model. In the social trust approach, p_j refers to the probability that a randomly chosen member of the reference group (e.g., a club, a neighborhood, or a country) is trustworthy in the same way that a specific individual was trustworthy in the basic model. While this is a minor change in the meaning of p, it is a significant change in the meaning of the concept. The trustor likely has less information about the average trustworthiness of a group than about specific, known individuals. At the lowest end of personal familiarity with the trustee, the trustor's estimate of p_j is simply an estimate of an average from some larger reference category $\bar{p}_j$.

The focus of the social trust tradition is the identification of the source and consequence of individuals' willingness to trust in their neighbors in a general sense. This approach focuses less on trustworthiness than dyadic approaches. Instead, the model imagines that trustors judge entire groups from which a trustee will be drawn. This may be as simple as whether a trustee believes a random draw of people from their club will walk away with cash that they left on the counter. This reference-category estimation process can make the process sound much like the institutional account that focuses on roles and identities.

The social trust approach has, more recently, blossomed into the investigation of trust as a resource that people and communities can deploy to accomplish their goals – social trust became social capital. Social capital merges the notion of social trust with the metaphor of capital to suggest that trust is a resource that people can use to accomplish their goals

(Fukuyama, 1996). A community with greater social capital may, for example, experience lower costs for surveillance and security or lower legal costs related to contract negotiations. The most famous proponent of the social capital approach, Robert Putnam, argued that the presence of social capital (or its decline) fundamentally shapes the community from individual interactions to the operations and processes of political organizations (1993; 2001).

This brief review of theories of social trust reveals the tension between the simple Coleman model that corresponds to common, daily decision-making and assessments of major political institutions. The next section turns to specific questions related to trust within the domain of politics. This shift will build on the foundation of the simple, interpersonal model of trust and the literature on broader social trust but take the models in new directions.

2.2 Political Trust

Research, particularly within political science, has investigated trust in political institutions rather than between individuals or between individuals and their neighbors. To some extent, this research tradition strains the metaphor of trust further even than the social trust literature. Whereas the foundational model of interpersonal trust involves a relationship between two specific agents and the model of social trust implied an assessment of average trustworthiness in a group, the literature on political trust investigates the relationship between a specific individual (the trustor) and a regime, institution, or organization as the trustee. This dramatically expands the scope of the trust decision, engaging larger risks (larger G and L) and less information on the trustworthiness of the trustee (p). The focus is, almost exclusively, on the attitudes of the trustor that may be related to the decision to report trust in a political regime, institution, or prominent individual.

As a trustor attitude, the research on trust in government generally links trust to fundamental concerns related to political legitimacy (Newton, Stolle, and Zmerli, 2018). The study of political theory has taken as a central concern the conditions under which the exercise of political power is justified. Why is it acceptable for government officials to do things that are not acceptable for individual people to do? For example, it is generally considered appropriate for a government to jail a criminal (hopefully following a fair trial). It is rarely considered acceptable for an individual to exercise such a power on their own – this would be tantamount to kidnapping. Rather, police powers are typically reserved for the state.

Most theories of political legitimacy are grounded in a theory of consent. The fundamental notion, associated with such thinkers as Hobbes, Locke, and

DeTocqueville (Newton, Stolle, and Zmerli, 2018), is that political authority derives from the consent of the governed. The police powers of the state, in particular, depend on the citizens[6] of the state accepting that the powers are acceptable. Of course, it is difficult to get individual consent from all people on all matters of political authority. Instead, these authors generally rely on a hypothetical exercise of consent. Would a reasonable person within a state agree with specific political authority? If so, general consent is presumed.

The question of legitimacy then turns to a consideration of what provides evidence that the citizenry still accept the legitimacy of their government. The clearest evidence is a general election. Specific votes provide strong evidence of consent to accept the rule of a particular regime. Of course, general elections are spaced out across time and leave few options to vocalize opposition to political authority in general. Interpretations of electoral results generally involve assessments of the specific individuals and regimes involved rather than assessments of the general apparatus of the state. This limits the usefulness of general elections as an indication of consent to the authority of an entire political system.

Some scholars sought an alternative to election results as an indication of consent for these reasons (Miller, 1974; Citrin, 1974). Similarly, David Easton investigated trust as a component of his broad systems model of political regimes (Easton, 1953). These scholars sought to learn what support there was for the entire political structure rather than for specific politicians or parties. In our review of the history of scholarship on trust in government, we saw a clear increase in the attention to trust in government in the midst of the Watergate scandal. Interest peaked as scholars wondered whether the negative assessments of the sitting president would erode sentiments about government more generally – and trust in government provided an attitude through which the scholars could assess this more general sentiment. Questions related to trust in government would give a sense of whether those critical of then President Nixon would blame him individually for the problems (or blame the network of people directly connected to the president) or whether there was a more general sense that all of the people involved in government and the process of government itself were problematic.

The broad assessment of trust in political systems has abandoned a fundamental part of the basic model of trust. Recall that fundamentally trust involves

---

[6] Most of these discussions use language related to citizenship but do not engage distinctions of status generated by an immigration system. We retain the use of the term "citizen" out of consistency with these historical roots but want to emphasize that the term "resident" may be a better parallel to the original discussions (Roberts, 2020).

some person trusting another person to perform a specific task. With systemic or regime-level studies of support for politics, there is rarely any specific task. It is hard to define what the ratio of $\frac{G}{L}$ even means in this context. Instead, questions solicited attitudes related to general performance and ideological alignment. Returning to the main subject of this study (trust in government), it is not clear what it means to have general trust in government. When someone reports a low level of trust in government, it may mean that there is a reduced set of commitments they expect the government will follow through on. This reduced set of commitments may be driven by changes in the assessment of the government (e.g., because of reduced capacity to follow through on commitments) or by changes in the acceptable consequences of a broken commitment. This brief discussion makes clear that it is hard to make a summary judgment of trust in government as a whole. It is not clear what the government is being trusted (or not trusted) to do. I may trust my neighbor to feed my pets but not to have access to my bank account. It is not enough to ask whether I trust my neighbor. I should ask whether I trust my neighbor for specific purposes. Similarly, investigations of trust in government that don't explain "trust the government to do what?" are frustratingly vague. This fundamental vagueness in the literature may explain the relatively low levels of attention that studies of trust in governments receive despite the general sense that there are important questions involved that may be tied to the very foundations of legitimate political authority.

And yet, there are reasons to believe that trust in government is an important resource for governance. Levi argues:

> The trustworthiness of the state influences its capacity to generate interpersonal trust, and the amount of socially and economically productive cooperation in the society in turn affects the state's capacity to govern. Trust of the state has additional consequences for governance: It affects both the level of citizen's tolerance of the regime and their degree of compliance with governmental demands and regulations. Destruction of trust may lead to widespread antagonism to government policy and even active resistance, and it may be one source of increased social distrust. (Levi, 1998, 87–88)

The development of legitimacy is not an idle concern. Consider the case of the pandemic: a loss of trust may lead to greater reluctance – or even active resistance – to policies intended to reduce the spread of COVID-19. Much of what the government does for pandemic response relies on the cooperation and compliance of its people to do things like avoid large gatherings and wear masks. As trust is destroyed, a space for reluctance and active resistance emerges.

Some of the most prominent work on the development of trust in the recent US case comes from Marc Hetherington's research into the dynamics of trust in the US government since the 1970s (Hetherington, 2005). Hetherington argues that the decline of trust in government (at a regime level) is responsible for significant alterations in the development of the American government. He begins by noting the patterns reviewed in the previous chapter of cycles of trust with a long-term declining trend since the 1970s, with exceptions of increasing trust during the first Reagan administration and the Clinton administration and in the aftermath of the 9/11 attacks. The increase following the 9/11 attacks was short-lived and followed by a similarly temporary bump in trust following the formal announcement of the Iraq War in 2002. The increased frequency of polling related to political trust allowed Hetherington to track these dynamics to an unprecedented degree.

Hetherington argues that trust is at the heart of a major transformation of the nature of the American political regime (Hetherington, 2005). He argues that trust, rather than changes in ideology or any conservative transformation of public opinion, explains major changes in American policy including the failures of health-care reform in the 1990s. Polling has not provided evidence of significant changes in political ideology over this period – though we have seen significant cycles of trust in government. Hetherington focuses on trust as a summary of a generalized evaluation of public policy – so, a decline in trust represents a generalized dissatisfaction with the regime. He writes:

> I define political trust as the degree to which people perceive that government is producing outcomes consistent with their expectations. One might think about it as a pragmatic running tally of how people think the government is doing at a given point in time. (2005, 9)

Hetherington uses the historical cycle of trust to make a startling argument about the nature of post-Watergate policymaking in the United States. He argues that the cycles of trust are more consistent with changes in policymaking than changes in ideology. Whereas scholars have sought (fruitlessly, Hetherington argues) to find the driver for a conservative turn in public opinion, Hetherington sees the change in reduced (but cycling) trust rather than any significant change in the ideology of the public.[7] More specifically, he argues that dissatisfaction with the large redistributive programs of the Great Society weakened trust in government and created a schism within the public (related, in part, to the racialized politics of redistributive policies) over the

---

[7] For a contrasting view, Chanley, Rudolph, and Rahn argue that trust in government is driven by economic factors, congressional scandals, and concerns about crime (2000).

effectiveness of these programs. Furthermore, this period defined redistributive politics as the frame through which people evaluated government. Together, the new frame and the dissatisfaction with redistributive politics led to declining trust. This decline in trust, then, transformed American policymaking in a way that decentered the state as the provider of services and brought along policy changes consistent with conservative ideology (even if there was little change in the ideology of the public over this time). Government became tied to its lowest-performing (in terms of trust) functions – while trust in other functions remained high.

Hetherington's argument connecting distrust to redistributive policies has important implications for the study of trust generally. Most importantly, this argument supports the contention that there is tremendous variety within a regime as to the trust placed in various organizations. While there may have been a decline in the trust in redistributive efforts, there are many non-redistributive policies that may not trigger the same levels of distrust. This argument is consistent with results from the Pew Foundation and others that, even amidst historic lows in the general trust in government measures (like those Hetherington focuses on), there were some agencies with remarkably high assessments, including the US Postal Service and the National Park Service (2019) – agencies with missions outside of problematic redistributive politics. It may matter less whether there is a high level of trust in government if there are high levels of trust in key functions.

We should ask, instead, what organizations and policies in government instill confidence and trust. Why do some organizations – like the US Postal Service and the National Park Service – get systematically and reliably higher evaluations? Hetherington's answer is that it depends on the nature of the service delivered. Both of these organizations are known, mostly, for their direct provision of services to the public. While both contain law enforcement functions that are, to some degree, redistributive (general tax funds support services only enjoyed by the people who take advantage of the programs), neither agency is thought of as primary redistributive. Rather, they are distributive as they are mostly defined by the services they provide.

Notice how far this research has wandered from the basic trust model. Hetherington's approach to studying trust in government is based on broad judgments about the adequacy of current public policy – rather than a specific delegation or a definable ratio of $\frac{G}{L}$. The literature on government trust became based on impressions of the government (particularly the federal government – a theme we will return to soon). It was not clear what the public trusted or failed to trust the government to do beyond a general antipathy for redistributive policies. As a result, we are currently in an all-time low of trust in government (generally) while also seeing high levels of support for specific agencies within that government.

We aspire to break through the ambiguity by investigating trust in government during the COVID-19 crisis while members of the public looked to specific agencies to help them in relatively specific ways. In the next section, we elaborate our strategy to investigate trust in government by investigating trust in specific administrative agencies involved in the COVID-19 response.

2.3 Trustworthiness and the Varieties of Agencies

The first element of our strategy is to investigate variation in the reported trust in specific administrative agencies (rather than the US government in general). If trust depends on the activities or commitments expected from the trusted agent, ambiguity in the activities or commitments are deeply problematic. Government, as a whole, conducts a wide variety of activities. A lack of trust could range from a concern for misappropriation of tax funds to a concern that police could kill you. It is hard to interpret what a specific stated level of trust implies about what a person fears (or expects) from the government.

Moving to the assessment of trust in a specific agency narrows the range of commitments and expectations from a specific trusted agent. If one is assessing a specific agency, one is assessing the activities typically carried out by that agency. Insofar as agencies have narrower ranges of activities, trust assessments of them are more clearly linked to specific activities. Trust in agencies known to provide regulatory oversight of the food supply, for example, will involve the willingness to accept the risk that the agency has not adequately prevented dangerous materials from entering our food. Statements about trust in this agency have a much clearer implication and a more likely connection to behavior than assessment of trust in general. A low level of trust in this regulatory agency is likely to lead to reluctance to buy food whose production is overseen by the agency. A high level of trust would lead to the expectation of a greater willingness or reduced hesitation to consume the food regulated by the agency. This approach is consistent with Heatherington's argument that trust is a function of the type of policy the public uses to evaluate a regime. Implicit in this argument is the notion that organizations that perform similar functions will report similar levels of trust, and those that differ in function will differ in trust.

The move to specific agencies does not completely eliminate uncertainty in the commitments and activities related to a specific agency. Some agencies may have more than one commonly understood activity. A local police office carries out patrols, jails offenders, and performs other activities. Each of these activities might have different consequences if performed ineffectively. However, even these agencies have a considerably narrowed range of activities and a clearer association of trust with related behaviors.

This book focuses on trust in agencies active as information providers (and in some cases, service providers) in the COVID-19 crisis. This narrows the range of activities that people are likely to consider as they consider the agencies under consideration. The book will focus on reported trust in organizations that members of the public are most likely to encounter as givers of advice during the pandemic. This narrowing of the range of activities avoids the most egregious of comparisons possible across a wider range of organizations – if we, for example, compared trust in the Internal Revenue Service (an organization that mostly interacts with residents in a negative context of audits and is implicated in the active redistribution of wealth) and the National Aeronautics and Space Administration (an organization with an indirect connection to most people).

There is some evidence that before the pandemic the Centers for Disease Control and Prevention (CDC) was highly regarded. Dan Carpenter compares trust in agencies across a variety of US agencies from a 2017 Gallup survey (Carpenter, 2019). He found that the CDC was behind only the US Postal Service in the proportion of respondents who reported "excellent/good" ratings of satisfaction. Furthermore, the CDC was one of the agencies with the lowest partisan gaps in this evaluation, with Republicans being only 4 percent more likely to report "excellent/good" ratings than Democrats. This provides a useful starting point in that at least the one health-focused organization for which we have data is a relatively highly regarded institution.

2.3.1 Trustworthiness and Federalism

In late March 2020, Statista released a poll of trust in information provided by a number of actors.[8] The top-rated organization was the US CDC with 85 percent reported trust. The survey then asked for general assessments of expertise from the "federal," "state," and "local" governments. These general categories were less trusted than the US CDC, with the state governments receiving the highest marks (70 percent) and local governments close behind (67 percent). The federal government trailed, with 53 percent reporting trust in their information. The gaps in support motivate our inclusion of organizations across the US federal system of policymaking.

---

[8] Watson, Amy. March 27, 2020. "Most trusted source of coronavirus news 2020." Statista. www.statista.com/statistics/1104557/coronavirus-trusted-news-sources-by-us.

The conventional account of trust in state and local governments is that people know so little about politics that these more local assessments are driven by their assessments of the federal government (Hetherington and Nugent, 2001; Uslaner, 2002). More recent work supports the proposition that when people are asked about specific state organizations, the assessments of these agencies are not entirely driven by trust in the federal government (Wolak and Palus, 2010; Banda and Kirkland, 2018). These results suggest that the strong relationship between trust in the federal government and trust in the state governments may be an artifact of the vague measurement approach of asking about a summary of an entire government rather than specific organizations that perform specific functions. Wolack has recently found that reporting of trust in state governments (still using the broad language) is a function of economic conditions, state political culture, and partisan control (relative to the respondent) as well as trust in the national government (2020).

While we limit our analysis to those actors and organizations most likely to provide information related to COVID-19 and personal safety (in contrast to the dominant approach of asking about regime or "whole of government" assessments), we have collected information on a wide range of organizations across our US federal policy system. From the federal level, this book will report on trust in the US Centers for Disease Control (US CDC) and the Department of Health and Human Services (HHS). These organizations have been among the most visible in advising the public on proper protective actions. Representatives from these organizations include Alex Azar (USs Secretary for Health and Human Services), Francis Collins (director of the National Institutes of Health (NIH)), Anthony Fauci (director of the National Institute of Allergy and Infectious Disease (NIAD)), and Robert Redfield (director of the US CDC). These are among the most visible and easily recognized national experts appearing in news reports. It is useful to note that the US CDC, the NIH, and the NIAD are all units within the HHS. The organizations studied here (the HHS and the US CDC) represent the federal organizations most active in providing information on COVID-19 and are the "faces" of the federal administrative agencies during the crisis.

State-level officials are also directly involved in COVID-19 response, from coordinating activities to providing information. State health departments, for example, are often the points of aggregation for information on state-level cases, deaths, etc. To represent state-level agencies involved in COVID-19, this book will discuss reported trust in "state health departments" and governors. Different states have different titles for their health agencies, so we opted for a more generic title. Governors have had a role in information dissemination in many states and here represent a more general indicator of the state government.

A variety of organizations operate at the local level as well. This Element focuses on two sets of actors and organizations: local hospitals and local physicians. This is also a case where varying local terminology makes uniform surveys across the United States challenging. In various jurisdictions, city or county offices may be more salient to respondents. To avoid this confusion, we asked more generally about local hospitals and local physicians/your primary care physician. The latter two options (local physicians/your primary care physician) are randomized, so that half of the respondents see one (and not the other).

This book will focus on six agencies relevant to COVID-19 response:

1. the US CDC
2. the HHS
3. (respondent's) state health department
4. (respondent's) governor
5. (respondent's) primary care physician (or) local physicians
6. local hospitals

A later section will review in more detail the design and implementation of the survey that collected the information for this Element.

Data on trust in these agencies allows us to compare the relative levels of trust across these organizations. These agencies vary in several ways, but a primary basis for their differences is in regards to their placement in our federal policy system. Conventionally, organizations thought to be further removed from respondents are expected to be less trusted by those respondents (Miller, 1974; Citrin, 1974). This expectation is grounded in the frequent observation that respondents typically report low levels of trust in "Congress" (a distant institution to most respondents) but higher levels of trust in their representatives in Congress. The elected officials that make up Congress have a connection to their constituents that renders the representatives "closer" to their constituents than the faceless aggregate institution that, to many, represents far-away, uncaring government. This rank-order is only roughly reflected in the data from Statista reported earlier. The state and local governments were similarly trusted for information on coronavirus (with state governments seeing slightly more trust). The federal government was noticeably behind.

A simple expectation based on these patterns is stated as hypothesis 1:

> *Hypothesis 1*: Trust in organizations decreases as the organization is farther removed (in the federal political system) from the respondent.

Hypothesis 1 is relatively simplistic. It would suggest three tiers of trust, with relatively similarity within each tier. Siegrist and colleagues argued that social trust and implied similarity of values were the strongest factor in explaining risk perceptions of new technologies (2000). It is important to note that the tradition from which Siegrist's research emerges is more closely related to social trust research than political trust research. This is a point where the social trust and political trusts reconnect for theoretical development though social trust researchers are generally less concerned about trust in specific actors or organizations. This salient value similarity hypothesis, coming from social trust research, reinforces the logic behind Hypothesis 1.

A second component of trust leads to contrasting expectations. Evidence suggests that people are more trusting of risk-related communications coming from actors and organizations seen as competent or expert (Eiser et al., 2009). This is consistent with recent work suggesting that party ownership of specific policy domains have led voters to assess the expertise and competency of parties in regards to these specific policies (Green and Jennings, 2017). Expertise is not evenly distributed through the organizations in this study. These differences are elided when one investigates only the regime level of "whole of government" trust. The regime-level approach ignores the tremendous variation reported in assessments of agencies as varied as the US CDC and the US IRS. The US CDC, in particular, is seen as a global leader on information related to infectious disease. This might explain the high levels of trust that Statista found in the US CDC compared to the more general "federal government." An expertise-based assessment would likely rank the US CDC as the most trusted. On the other end of the spectrum, governors typically have limited subject-matter expertise related to COVID-19. They are political generalists who rely on messages of value similarity to win elections. The same, to a lesser extent, applies to the more general US HHS. Within each the federal tier, we would expect expert agencies (the US CDC and state health departments) to be more trusted than their more general counterparts (the US HHS and governors, respectively). This consideration leads to some contrasting expectations presented in Hypothesis 2:

> *Hypothesis 2*: Within a level of federalism, trust in organizations will be higher for agencies that are known for their expertise relevant to COVID-19 than for generalist organizations.

These initial hypotheses provide a useful starting point for investigating variation in trust in organizations involved in COVID-19 response. However, they represent only a partial view of the importance of trust. These initial hypotheses focus on how characteristics of the organization (position in the federal system, presumed expertise) affect levels of reported trust. However, there are also characteristics of the respondents that may influence how those respondents assess various agencies. Research "has given scant support for the hypotheses that demography plays a significant role in political trust (Listhaug and Jakobsen, 2017, 561). Listhaug and Jakobsen argue, though, that the lack of evidence is due to how demographics only affect political trust when linked to specific conflicts and controversies.

This Element focuses on two of the more prominent respondent characteristics that are often thought to influence trust in government, some of which are particularly salient in regards to COVID-19 response. The most prominent of these is party identification (Keele, 2005). Scholars of public opinion often consider party identification to be a fundamental characteristic of respondents and the basis by which they often generate more specific attitudes. Party identification may, for example, be the basis for people to decide whether they support a specific policy. If the respondent is not sure about a specific new policy, they are likely to fall back on signals from the preferred political party for guidance on whether they should support or oppose the policy. While it is clearly the case that people within political parties vary in their support of different policies, there is a great deal of consistency within the party. For this reason, it is a starting point for examining how respondent characteristics affect trust in government. This leads us to Hypothesis 3:

> *Hypothesis 3* Trust in organizations will vary based on respondents' reported party affiliation.

The second respondent characteristic that this volume will investigate is respondent age. This variable has particular salience in an investigation related to COVID-19. While there was a great deal of uncertainty about the nature of COVID-19 at the starting point of the surveys reported here (March 2020), it was widely known that COVID-19 has the greatest effect on older people. This makes issues related to COVID-19, and the organizations poised to respond to the pandemic, of particular importance for older respondents. This leads to Hypothesis 4:

> *Hypothesis 4* Trust in organizations will vary based on respondents' reported age.

This Element will discuss these hypotheses individually as well as part of a multivariate model to assess the joint contributions of these issues and to control for potential confounding relationships (such as with gender, race, or risk perception of COVID-19). We will discuss these factors in more detail when we investigate the relationship between each factor and respondent trust.

These hypotheses motivate the remainder of this Element. The next section will present our approach to collecting data to test these hypotheses. The following sections will move through the assessment of the hypotheses presented already – sometimes specifying them in greater detail.

3 Data Collection

The onset of the COVID-19 crisis brought a flood of reporting and information – often with conflicting advice, setting off debates about whom to believe. This Element reports on evidence related to trust in actors and organizations relevant to COVID-19 response early in the crisis. Coming in to March 2020, there were concerns about COVID-19 expanding from its initial outbreak location of China into several other nations. On March 2, the US CDC reported forty-three "confirmed or suspected cases" in ten US states. Agencies and attentive publics were growing concerned but largely considered the risk, at the moment, to be low. Within a couple of weeks, matters had changed entirely. Travel restrictions were becoming almost universal, and variations on "safer-at-home" were becoming commonplace. Within these weeks, the world had changed. It is not surprising that people were clamoring for information in these circumstances.

The National Institute for Risk and Resilience (NIRR) at the University of Oklahoma routinely monitors the discussion of major risks on Twitter. In early January, as discussion of the outbreak and Wuhan heated up, the NIRR began daily monitoring reports on Twitter activity. In February, it became clear that COVID-19 warranted special attention. By late February, a team assembled through the NIRR began assembling a survey instrument intended for a broad public survey on issues related to COVID-19. The team gathered or wrote questions related to risk assessment, trust in relevant agencies, and support for protective actions and policies. This speed was essential to getting the instrument into the field quickly at the earliest stages of what would become a national and global crisis. After designing the instrument, the survey went into the field in mid-March at the earliest stages of the aggressive response across most of the country.

This section will describe the process of creating the survey and the choices that went into the process.

3.1 Survey Sample

The intention of the survey is to provide a broad and representative view of the American public's views of the risks of COVID-19 and several related issues. There is a focus on respondents' views of trust and intentions to take protective actions. The starting point is to develop a sample of survey respondents that permits this view and avoids the dangers of ignoring large segments of the population or exaggerating the prominence of other segments.

To gather such a sample required careful management. The NIRR contracted with Qualtrics to access a panel of internet-based respondents. The panel involves an active process of monitoring to ensure that the resulting sample includes a mix of respondents that will resemble the population of the United States. This process is the emerging standard to ensure representativeness where a census and random sampling is not possible (Berrens et al., 2003).

The result of this process is a sample of 1,000 respondents each month (250 respondents a week) who broadly resemble the United States as a whole (the exact count depends on how difficult it is to recruit a properly balanced sample for any given week). This Element will first discuss the results from March 2020 in detail – to establish a firm baseline. A later section will compare the results from March to results from the weekly samples from April through November.[9] Table 1 provides a comparison of our March sample proportions of various demographic groups within the survey sample and census estimates of the same categories.

Table 1 reveals that the sampling strategy has successfully created a sample that closely resembles the diversity of the United States in several key respects. The gender proportion is almost identical in the two estimates. The racial distribution is close with the survey sample, having a slightly lower proportion of white and Hispanic respondents with slightly higher proportion of Black respondents. Across age groups, the two samples are also similar, with each proportion being within 2 percentages of each other. The sample also includes balance across US regions (Midwest, Northwest, South, and West). These similarities are particularly important for the demographic characteristics that we investigate in detail later in the study, including age. The regional balance is important as regional adjustments to COVID-19 varied widely while the survey was in the field.

The close match of the sample characteristics to census estimates gives us confidence that patterns we observe within the sample represent patterns also present in the general US population. There are always concerns that differences between the sample and the population on unmeasured variables could

---

[9] Our survey months do not align perfectly with the calendar months. The March survey ran six days into April, for example. The first/March sample ran for twenty-one days, while the others all ran for twenty-eight to twenty-nine days. Keeping the windows equal in length introduced some drift, such that, by the end of the year, the months were misaligned with calendar months. For this reason, we report on sequentially numbered months (of twenty-eight to twenty-nine days) rather than month names after March.

Table 1 Demographic representation

Statistic	Sample Estimate	Census Estimate
Male	49.1%	48.7%
Female	50.9%	51.3%
White	73.3%	77.9%
Black	12.7%	13.0%
Other Race	14.0%	9.1%
Hispanic	18.5%	16.3%
Non-Hispanic	81.5%	83.7%
Age 18–34	30.5%	30.0%
Age 35–59	42.5%	41.3%
Age 60+	27.1%	28.7%
Midwest	20.7%	20.8%
Northeast	17.1%	17.2%
South	38.2%	38.4%
West	23.9%	24.0%

lead to hasty inferences. However, the key suspects for a lack of representativeness (gender, race, age, and region) are absent here. This sample does seem to resemble the population from which it is drawn. Based on this close correspondence between the sample and the population on the observable measures, we are confident in our ability to use standard hypothesis testing procedures to assess differences within our sample and to argue that such differences reflect differences within the population.

3.2 Instrument Design

The NIRR built a survey instrument based on its extensive experience with survey design. It is essential to keep in mind the timing of the survey design and implementation. The survey was in the field while there was a great deal of uncertainty about the nature of threat presented by COVID-19. After some basic demographic questions on age, education, gender, race, and region, the survey turns to a battery of questions about risk perceptions related to COVID-19 and questions of knowledge of COVID-19 and sources of information.

Following questions about policy support and risk perception, the survey includes assessments of trust in various relevant organizations. Questions assessing trust come in a variety of forms. The question battery from the National Election Study has included as many as five questions about "trust in government" (generally), but the battery has been modified over time to include as few as two components. The result is what a NES Pilot Study referred to as a "mishmash" of approaches (Gershtenson, Ladewig, and Plane, 2006).

Having multiple questions to assess trust is attractive but can be problematic when moving from the assessment of "trust in government" (generally) to the assessment of trust in specific agencies. The survey would quickly bloat with four questions related to trust for every organization used in the study. Economy in question wording was particularly important as the survey design included preparations for follow-up studies. Committing to multiple questions for every agency proved to be untenable. Instead, the survey includes a single, direct question stem applied to a list of organizations and people.

The basic trust questions stem states:

> Issues concerning potential health risks are often complex. Please indicate the level of trust you have in experts on public health issues from the following organizations:

The survey directs respondents to assess their "level of trust" with special emphasis on trust in "experts on public health issues." This wording is intended to help focus the assessment based on the theory of trust discussed in the previous sections, including elements of expertise. The focus of the question on trust in relation to expertise helps stabilize responses within the need to combine four (or more) component questions.

The survey then provides the following actors and organizations for assessment based on the previous trust question stem:

- The US Centers for Disease Control (US CDC)
- The US Department of Health and Human Services (HHS)
- The World Health Organization (WHO)
- The [respondent's state] State Health Department
- Local ambulance services and emergency medical technicians (EMTs)
- Pharmaceutical companies
- (randomized) Your primary care physician/Local physicians
- Local hospitals
- State and local news or media
- National news or media
- The governor of [respondent's state]

Given our interests in federalism, this Element will not discuss the results for private companies (including media) or international organizations. We will also not discuss the results for ambulance services and emergency medical technicians (EMTs) to simplify the discussion of local health providers.

The results of this survey provide information on how members of a representative sample of residents of the United States rate six actors and organizations relevant to COVID-19 response in terms of trust as well as the respondents' intentions to take specific protective actions. The Element will use these data to provide a view of how trust in these organizations – both across the federal system and across various respondent characteristics – and these attitudes changed over time throughout the pandemic. The results begin in the next section.

4 Variation in Trust

Our most basic question is to what extent people in the United States trust actors and organizations taking major roles in COVID-19 response. This section provides an overview of the reported trust in a variety of organizations across different levels of federalism in March 2020. The section begins with a series of simple reviews of the levels of trust in each actor and organization. These simple reviews provide a sense of the overall reputation of these agencies without comparing levels of trust across different social groups. The review will conclude with an assessment of the combined influence of party identification, age, level of concern regarding COVID-19, and other factors that might influence a respondent's reported level of trust in health agencies.

The next section compares the levels of trust reported by different social groups in the United States – notably, political party identifiers and different age groups. As argued in an earlier section, these groups are either particularly likely to have contrasting views of trust (in the case of party identification) or to have particular vulnerabilities to COVID-19 that make matters of trust in actors and organizations particularly salient.

4.1 Variation across US Agencies: US CDC, HHS, State Health Departments, Governors, and Local Providers

The starting point for our investigation is to look at the basic results for our respondents' trust in organizations relevant to COVID-19 response in March 2020. Figure 2 visualizes the mean level of trust for each of the organizations in the study.

There are two lessons embedded within Figure 2. First, the organizations have relatively similar levels of trust. As further investigation will reveal, the averages conceal interesting differences between the levels of trust in these organizations. However, the average similarity stands out. Second, the level of trust is relatively high – between 3.5 and 4.0 on a five-point scale. This contrasts with previous discussion of the low levels of "trust in government" and reported

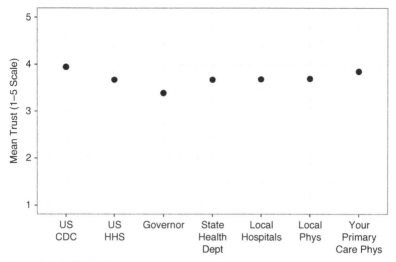

Figure 2 Similarity in trust across agencies involved in COVID-19 response

evaluations of such institutions as Congress. Surveys asking about "trust in government" routinely find percentages in the 20s reporting this trust. The results for health-specific organizations are considerably more positive (though the underlying metrics and questions are quite different). We will return to the comparison of averages after specific discussions of the reported trust in each organization. Future visual comparisons of all of the organizations will focus on the range of relevant variation rather than this full range, so that we can see where differences between the reported trust are statistically significant.

This review will start with some of the more notable federal agencies involved in pandemic response. The most prominent in the public's eye is the US CDC. The US CDC is one of the most prominent organizations in media coverage of the COVID-19 pandemic. The US CDC was seen as the subject-matter expert specific to infectious diseases like the SARS-COV-2 virus that causes COVID-19. The assessments of the US CDC represent a useful baseline for what a highly trusted and highly expert agency can expect in terms of trust assessments.

The results, reported in Table 2, confirm the general sense that the US CDC is a highly trusted organization. The top two categories of trust ("high trust" and "complete trust") include 1,487 respondents, with only 103 respondents reporting "low" or "no" trust in the US CDC (7 percent). Note that these results indicate eleven times as many people are in our two highest trust categories than are in the lowest two categories. Watching the relative portion of the highest two and the lowest two categories will be a useful way to consider the distribution of responses across all of the options – beyond the simple means. A normally

Table 2 Reported trust in the US CDC

	No Trust	Low Trust	Moderate Trust	High Trust	Complete Trust
n	33	70	351	525	506
%	(2.2%)	(4.7%)	(24%)	(35%)	(34%)

Table 3 Reported trust in the US HHS

	No Trust	Low Trust	Moderate Trust	High Trust	Complete Trust
n	53	106	466	517	345
%	(3.6%)	(7.1%)	(31%)	(35%)	(23%)

distributed variable would be symmetrical around the mean, with equal proportions in the highest and lowest categories. The observed ratio represents a tremendous skew towards high levels of trust for the US CDC.

The US Department of Health and Human Services (HHS) is the larger cabinet-level department that includes a variety of organizations involved in COVID-19 response including the US CDC and other health-related organizations. The HHS is the central planning organization for federal COVID-19 efforts and represents a more general assessment of federal efforts related to the pandemic.

Table 3 provides the trust assessments for the HHS from our respondents. The level of trust for HHS is strong with 862 respondents giving the HHS one of the two highest trust assessments (58 percent) with only 159 respondents giving it one of the lowest two trust assessments (11 percent). The resulting ratio is 5.2 times more respondents in the highest categories relative to lower categories.

Figure 3 illustrates the levels of trust in these two federal agencies. From the figure, it is clear that the trust in these two agencies is quite similar. There is a preponderance of assessments at similarly high levels across the two agencies. The largest difference is that fewer people report "complete trust" in the HHS than in the US CDC. Overall, this seems to be a strong level of trust for two of the most important federal providers of information related to COVID-19.

Trust in state organizations is more varied. State health departments receive a similar level of support to what we have seen with the two federal agencies. Table 4 reports the assessments of trust in the state health departments. The survey asked each respondent to rate their own state health department

Table 4 Reported trust in the state health departments

	No Trust	Low Trust	Moderate Trust	High Trust	Complete Trust
n	50	107	461	536	333
%	(3.4%)	(7.2%)	(31%)	(36%)	(22%)

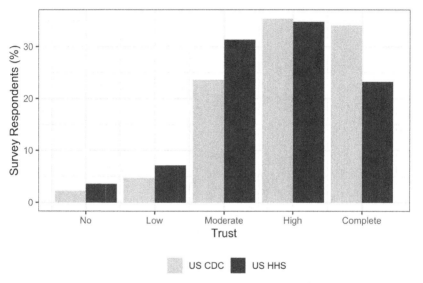

Figure 3 Reported trust in the US CDC and the HHS

(with their state in the question and drawn from the respondent's prior response about their home state – for example, a respondent who said she was from Colorado would be asked about Colorado's state health department). The distribution of trust is quite similar, specifically, to the assessments of the HHS – without the larger number of "complete trust" responses seen with the US CDC. In the case of state health departments, the "high trust"/"low trust" ratio is 5.5 - a similar skew to the US HHS.

Governors received less support than the administrative agencies assessed so far. As with state health agencies, respondents were asked to specifically assess their own state's governor. Table 5 reports the distribution of responses. The governors are seeing much more frequent reports of low levels of trust ("no trust" or "low trust") and much less frequent reports of the highest levels of trust ("high trust" and "complete trust"). As a result, the governors only see a 2.4 ratio of high to low trust responses.

Figure 4 illustrates the assessments for both state-level actors and organizations side by side. The comparison makes the difference between the relatively

Table 5 Reported trust in governors

	No Trust	Low Trust	Moderate Trust	High Trust	Complete Trust
n	127	168	492	401	297
%	(8.6%)	(11%)	(33%)	(27%)	(20%)

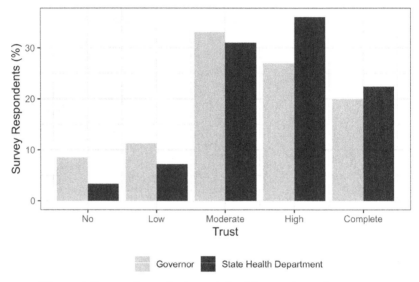

Figure 4 Reported trust in the state health agencies and governors

highly trusted state health agencies and the state governors clearer. The differences are not so stark as when comparing a distrusted organization to a trusted one; they are notable, though. There are differences in the lower levels of trust and in terms of "high trust." Interestingly, the difference between these organizations is not as large for reports of "complete trust." The administrative agency is trusted more than the elected executive in the state. This alone could inspire consideration related to whom should be making state-level recommendations if the recommendations are intended to maximize compliance or acceptance.

The final set of actors and organizations are those at the local level. These actors and organizations include a more heterogeneous set of organizations. Our analysis compares the assessed trust in local hospitals and local physicians (asked both regarding one's own primary care physicians and local physicians generically). These actors include representatives from the private sector, nonprofit organizations, and the government sector. It is important to recall that the traditional literature on trust suggests that the closer organizations are to an

Table 6 Reported trust in local hospitals

	No Trust	Low Trust	Moderate Trust	High Trust	Complete Trust
n	46	106	482	499	354
%	(3.1%)	(7.2%)	(32%)	(34%)	(24%)

Table 7 Reported trust in local physicians

	No Trust	Low Trust	Moderate Trust	High Trust	Complete Trust
n	42	77	444	539	380
%	(2.8%)	(5.2%)	(30%)	(36%)	(26%)

assessor, the higher the expected rating of trust. This influence of closeness, though, is offset to some degree by a simultaneous premium on expertise.

Local hospitals are well regarded – in a manner similar to the results for the federal agencies and state health agencies. Table 6 reports the specific distribution. Local hospitals see few reports of the lowest levels of trust and many more of the higher levels of trust: specifically, only 152 responses in the lowest two categories compared to 854 at the two highest levels (a ratio of 5.6). This difference is not as large as the almost ten-fold difference for the US CDC but is similar to the reports for the HHS.

Local physicians receive similar levels of support. Table 7 reports these results. Local physicians receive only 119 responses in the two lowest categories, with 919 in the two highest categories.[10] This ratio of 7.75 is the best outside of the US CDC. These raw results may defy some expectations. Our two highest-rated agencies in terms of the difference between highest and lowest ratings are a distant federal agency with little direct contact with residents and the most local, most personal group of local physicians. Distance is important – but it only tells part of the story. Especially in a case like this where the trust assessment includes a prominent component of technical expertise, trust is distributed unevenly across the federal system.

The local organizations are quite similar to each other (and similar to what we saw with the state health departments and the HHS). Figure 5 presents the

---

[10] It is important to note that this measure combines two questions. We asked half of the sample about "local physicians" and half about "your local physician." We report the raw numbers of the combined question in Figure 7 but compare the two versions in the final figure.

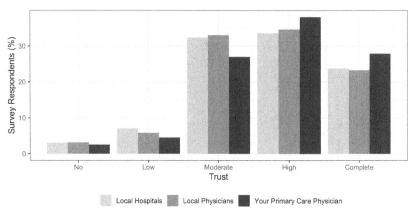

Figure 5 Reported trust in the local hospitals and physicians

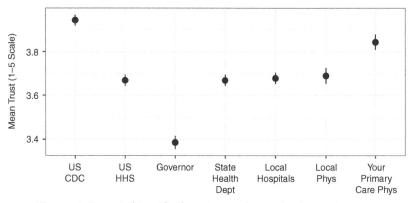

Figure 6 Reported trust in the actors and organizations relevant to COVID-19 response

trust assessments of the two local agencies for side-by-side comparison. There is more trust for one's own primary care physician – as the distance hypotheses would suggest. Hospitals and local physicians (generally) are quite similar, though.

Figure 6 provides a final comparison of all of these organizations for comparison (with standard deviations represented with bars). For ease of comparison, this figure only includes the means and standard deviations of the trust assessments – not the count at each level as in the earlier tables. The range of the figure focuses on the relevant range of variation, so that the standard deviations are visible and the three tiers become easier to differentiate. The comparison renders vivid the similarity between the different groups of organizations. The US CDC is clearly the most trusted agency in the group. This is followed by respondent's own primary care physicians. The personal physician is followed by a cluster of organizations including the HHS, state health agencies, local hospitals, and local (not one's own) physicians. These organizations are statistically indistinguishable from each other in terms of their average levels of support.

The final organization is the state governors. They have the lowest average rating by a substantial margin (more than .2 on the scale – which is just less than the difference between the US CDC and the cluster of four organizations). The governors should be in the middle if assessments are based on a simple version of the distance hypothesis. The governors also have what should be an advantage with familiarity, based on their selection as a result of popular elections. This direct electoral connection to their electorate is not enough to buoy their trust assessments. This may be a case of an organization not known for expertise losing trust for that reason. The other organizations are health-specific whereas the governors are generalists. This supports the contention that expertise – maybe within a specifically relevant domain – is an important contributor to the trust assessments.

It is important to note that the state governors and their associated state agencies vary in the partisan identification – unlike the federal agencies which were controlled by the Republican party throughout our survey period. Just over half of the governors were Republicans in 2020, but that means that some respondents were assuming Republican governors while others were assuming their own Democratic governors. We will discuss this complication when we drill further into issues related to party identification.

This general discussion creates a baseline for the trust assessments in the various organizations we study as relevant to COVID-19 response. There is variation in the levels of trust in different organizations. Distance (in the form of the federal hierarchy) does not explain the pattern exceptionally well. Rather, an expert organization stands out of the central cluster of organizations (the US CDC), one local organization stands out as having higher ratings than the central clusters (personal physicians), and governors fall well behind the others, being both moderately distant (as a state-level official) and not possessing health-specific expertise. Expertise explains this pattern better than distance – but there is reason to believe that both components are operating.

4.2 Variations in Trust across Party Identity

4.2.1 Party Identification and Trust in Agencies

Party identification has been a central concept in the study of US politics and public opinion for decades. The dominant approach is to consider party affiliation as foundational while more specific attitudes are derived from this foundation. For example, the typical explanation for opinions on specific policy controversies (like whether to close businesses to prevent the spread of COVID-19) is that people will look to the leaders of the chosen political party for cues. When parties disagree, we would expect to see divergence of opinions among the public based on party affiliation. Party identification has specifically strong ties with assessments of trust in government (Keele, 2005).

During the COVID-19 pandemic, the most common topic in the media related to party affiliation was how Democrats and Republicans had very different reactions to policy options such as closing businesses, limiting travel, and other policy options. Less often, one would hear concerns that Republicans were unwilling to listen to medical advice from "Washington bureaucrats" and would refuse to take personal protective actions themselves, like wearing masks. The most dramatic of these claims were based on a CBS poll from late March (in the field at around the time of our March sample) that found more Republicans trusted President Trump for medical advice than reported they trusted the US CDC for this advice. Conversely, very few Democrats reported trusting the president for this advice, while more trusted the US CDC. Those reading more closely saw that the variation was largely over the trust in the president but that the differences in the trust in the CDC was only about a 10% difference.[11] The survey will reveal more about partisan differences in trust early in the crisis.

4.2.2 Comparison of Trust across Party Identification

Figure 7 illustrates the variations in reported trust in federal health agencies related to COVID-19 response across different party identifiers. What stands out immediately from the figure is how similar Democrats and Republicans are – but how major party independents report lower levels of trust.[12] The lowest levels of trust are hard to distinguish based on the figure, but it is easy to see that party independents reported "low" trust at much greater frequencies than

---

[11] Haltiwanger, John. March 25, 2020. "Republicans trust Trump more than the CDC for accurate info on the coronavirus, a new poll shows." *Business Insider*. www.businessinsider.com/republicans-trust-trump-more-than-cdc-coronavirus-new-poll-shows-2020-3.

[12] It is important to note that major party independents are a diverse group. This group includes Green Party members, Libertarian Party members, and others, including those who do not identify with any party. The number of people who identify with these smaller parties is not large enough to support differentiated comparison to the memberships of the two major parties. Even the largest of these non-major parties represent fewer than a hundred respondents and cannot support statistical comparisons. Naturally, the differentiation of major party independents would be interesting but would require a more targeted data collection strategy. This limitation, however, leads us to refer to people who do not identify as members of the Democratic and Republican parties as major party independents.

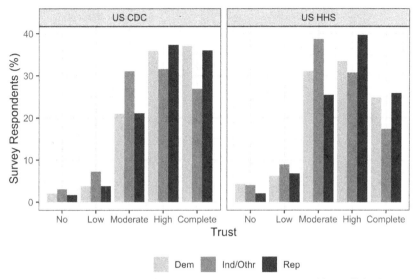

Figure 7 Reported trust in the US CDC and HHS separated by political party affiliation

both Democrats and Republicans. Major party independents were also nota-bly more likely to report moderate levels of trust rather than the higher levels seen for identifiers with either major party. The greater frequencies of low and moderate trust result in lower frequencies of the highest two categories of trust compared to major party identifiers.

These results may surprise readers who expect to see major differences in political attitudes to map onto party differences. The results here suggest something quite different was going on in March 2020. Both Democrats and Republicans reported similarly high levels of trust in both the US CDC and the HHS. There are two potential surprises to unpack. First, the comparison across the major parties is not between one who trusts the US CDC and one who does not (or does so at a low level). Members of both parties report high levels of trust in the agency even though the agency is part of a Republican administration.

The second surprise is that the major party independents report noticeably lower levels of trust in both the US CDC and the HHS than either group of party identifiers. The key difference is between major party identifiers and non-identifiers – not between identifiers of the two major parties. It is tempt-ing for people to expect major party independents to be a moderate category between two parties representing two poles of an ideological divide. This vision is not supported in this case. The non-identifiers don't have a moderate position between the parties – the major party independents are the outliers (compared to both parties) in regards to trust in the federal agencies. This suggests that major

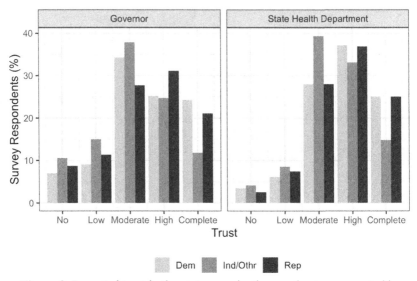

Figure 8 Reported trust in the state organizations and actors separated by political party affiliation

party independents are not in a transitional state between two party-based perspectives (at least in regards to trust to these agencies) but represent a different category altogether.

Major party independents stand out as having particularly low levels of trust in state organizations and actors as well. Figures 8 illustrates these patterns. We see in this figure greater proportions of the major party independents at the lowest levels of trust and remarkably lower proportions of independents reporting "complete trust" in these actors. Again, the major party independents stand out as their own, low-trust grouping rather than as a transitional group between Republicans and Democrats.

It is natural to wonder whether trust is driven largely by a party match between a respondent and their governor's party – rather than the parties having their own levels of trust (irrespective of the party in control of the state). The state agencies provide a useful opportunity to contrast the influence of party membership and the influence of match (or mismatch) between a respondent and their own state government. There is some evidence that the party match influence is strong. Figure 9 illustrates this comparison. Respondents with matching party affiliations are more likely to report higher levels of trust in their governor and state health department. This approach is difficult to interpret as there are no matching state parties to represent the major party independents. There is evidence of a matching effect that supports a value similarity interpretation of trust. Matching state governments are closer, in ideological terms, and thus more trusted.

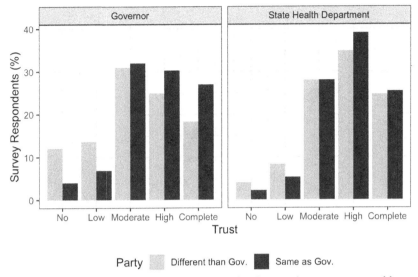

Figure 9 Reported trust in the state organizations and actors separated by political party match

Figure 10 completes the set of comparisons for the local actors and organizations. At the broadest level, the patterns remain the same. Major party independents are the least trusting group, with higher proportions of low trust responses and lower proportions of the highest levels. What is most notable here, though, is that the low levels of trust reported by major party independents hold even for personal physicians. The levels of trust in personal physicians are higher than other organizations among major party independents, but the lower level of trust (compared to partisans) still holds in this case. These personal physicians are not typically governmental actors and are about as "close" to the respondents as a health information provider can be. Even here, major party independents stand out from major party identifiers (both Republicans and Democrats) – suggesting that major party independents are not merely distrusting of government organizations. The major party independents are comparatively less trusting than major party identifiers across the board.

The lesson from the comparison of major party identifiers and trust in organizations and actors relevant to COVID-19 is that the relatively high levels of trust – and the consistency in their scores – conceal a great deal of systematic variation. Trust levels vary systematically across party identification (and party match when that is possible to contrast) but not in the way that many might suspect. Instead, major partisan independents emerge as particularly low in trust rather than a transitional or moderate state between the two major parties. Trust in government is clearly caught in the party dynamics of our polarized era but

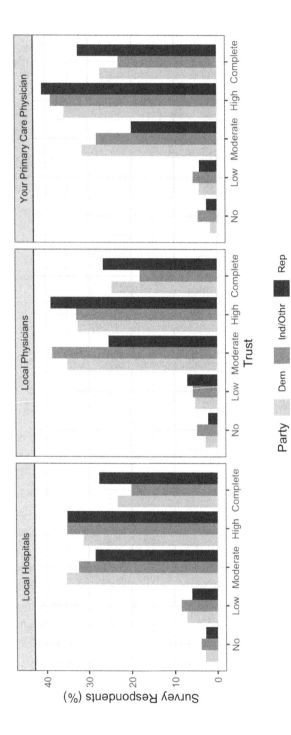

Figure 10 Reported trust in the local organizations and actors separated by political party affiliation

not strictly along party lines – though the party match evidence suggests that there is a gap between in-party and out-party members in the states.

The characterization of major party independents is quite difficult. Their diversity and small numbers make it hard to assess their place in a US national sample. Future work could focus on major party independents to assess whether major party independents are a coherent group that rejects the major parties or is a heterogeneous category that includes high-trust and low-trust members that map to specific minor parties. For example, it may be the case that Libertarians have lower-than-average trust while Green Party members have a higher trust than average. Pooling a heterogeneous group would likely result in moderate trust assessments, which is not what we see. Pooling major party independents may conceal such patterns, but a sample of this design can not reliably assess such differences.

4.3 Variations across Age

While party identification has been a key subject of study in public opinion, age is a key distinction in regards to the specific threat presented by COVID-19. Early into the crisis, and before the survey reported here, the US CDC and the World Health Organization (WHO) emphasized that older people were at far greater risk of death if they contracted COVID-19. Reports proliferated that hospitalizations for COVID-19 ran particularly high among older victims and the probability was higher that older hospitalized patients would require extreme therapeutic techniques like long-term respirator use. From March and for months after, the CDC maintained its statement that anyone over the age of sixty-five is particularly vulnerable and should take extraordinary steps to protect themselves, including complete isolation at home.

4.3.1 Age and Trust in Agencies

Age has proven to be an important component of prior models of trust in administrative agencies (Robinson, Stoutenborough, and Vedlitz, 2017). There is an emerging pattern suggesting that older residents report higher levels of trust, more or less across the board. The causal mechanism behind this pattern is unclear – though subject to some speculation. To the extent that trust is the product of repeated interaction, having a long series of experiences may build trust over time. Individual interactions with administrative agencies are more likely to be negative when younger (when the primary points of contact are with teachers, law enforcement, and case workers). Over time, these interactions may build toward trust, especially as people move to ages where they take advantage of more universally positive experiences like social security and Medicare.

These general tendencies layer on top of the increased salience of COVID-19 for older respondents. Together these considerations lead us to expect that older respondents will report higher levels of trust across the actors and organizations considered here. The literature does not provide a strong reason to expect that this expectation should vary across different organizations.

4.3.2 Comparison of Trust across Age

To visualize changes in trust across different age groups, we focus on two particular groups. One group, representing relatively young respondents, includes the respondents reporting being between eighteen and thirty-four years old. This young group contrasts with an older group of respondents reporting their age as being at or above sixty years. This provides a comparison of two large segments of the samples – one the youngest in the sample and one the oldest. The exclusion of the respondents in the middle allows for a clearer comparison of differences.

Figure 11 presents the comparison of younger and older respondents' trust assessments for our selected federal agencies. Some of the pattern is familiar from the overall distribution. Overall, older respondents report higher levels of trust in the federal agencies. Younger respondents are more likely to report the lowest two levels of trust, while the older respondents are more likely to report the highest two levels of trust. This holds across both the US CDC and the HHS. It is also interesting that the higher levels of "complete trust" observed in the

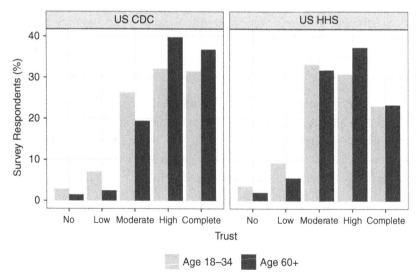

Figure 11 Reported trust in the US CDC and the HHS separated by age

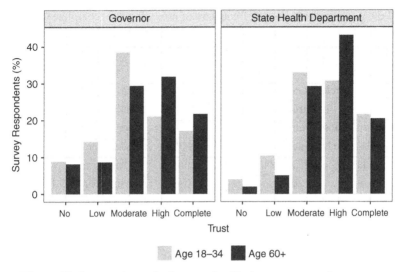

Figure 12 Reported trust in the state health departments and governors
separated by age

overall numbers are replicated here for both the older and younger groups. That
is, both groups are more likely to rate the US CDC at the highest level of trust
than the HHS.

The comparison of age groups for state organizations is more complicated
(see Figure 12). For governors, the older respondents are more trusting as
expected. Younger respondents have noticeably higher levels of both lower
categories of trust and lower frequency of reporting the highest levels of trust.
The younger age group reports trust that is quasi-normally distributed with the
modal response of "moderate" trust and only a slight skew toward more higher
levels of reported trust than lower than "moderate." The older respondents actually have a modal response of "high trust" (but not with a large difference
between "high" and "moderate" trust) and a strong skew toward higher trust
categories.

The patterns for state health departments is more complicated. There is,
again, a general skew toward positive trust evaluations – certainly compared
to the assessments of governors. For both groups, there are far more responses
in the two high categories than the two low categories. It is again the case that
the younger respondents are more likely than older respondents to report the
two lower levels of trust. The patterns within the high levels of trust, though, are
somewhat different than what we have seen before. The older respondents are
much more likely to report a "high" level of trust than the younger respondents.
However, the younger respondents are slightly more likely to give the highest
rating for trust than their older counterparts. The differences between younger

and older respondents in their frequency of providing the "complete trust" is small, but it is an unusual case of the older respondents not being more trusting than the younger counterparts. This may reflect different likely experiences with the state health agencies themselves.

Local agencies received strong support, as expected. Figure 13 illustrates these results. The trust assessments for older respondents are consistently higher than those from their younger counterparts. Here some of the gaps are larger than we have seen at previous levels of government. For local hospitals, the modal response for younger respondents is only "moderate" trust while the mode for older respondents is "high trust." The same patterns holds for local physicians (not personal physicians). This is reflective of a higher level of trust among older respondents. The distribution related to personal physicians (the prompt that specifies a respondent's own physician, rather than merely "local" physicians) supports the suspicion that some of the trust evaluations may be driven by repeated interaction opportunities. The younger respondents are less likely to have repeated and consistent interactions with their own physician. For younger respondents, there is a slightly higher level of trust for their own physician, but this increase is much larger for older respondents. For older respondents, they are about as likely to report "high" trust as "complete trust." It is plausible that this is driven by the likely more frequent interaction between older respondents and their personal physicians.

The potential for higher levels of trust with repeated interaction creates the possibility of asymmetric relations between these interactions and trust. The lowest two levels of trust are consistent among older respondents across both the general local physician and their personal physician. The major differences between these two cases for older respondents is between the highest two levels of trust. It may be that repeated interactions like these have the greatest effect on the highest levels of trust. It may be, then, that the ideal strategies for digging an agency out of the lowest levels of trust are different than the ideal strategies for building trust from moderate to higher levels. This is a topic only suggested by the evidence presented here but warrants careful thought and future investigation.

4.4 A Multivariate Model of Trust in Health Information Providers

The preceding analysis focused on bivariate analyses of potential correlates of trust in agents and organizations providing health information related to COVID-19. While interesting, these bivariate comparisons are simplistic. The results indicated that expected ratings for trust increased as the age of the

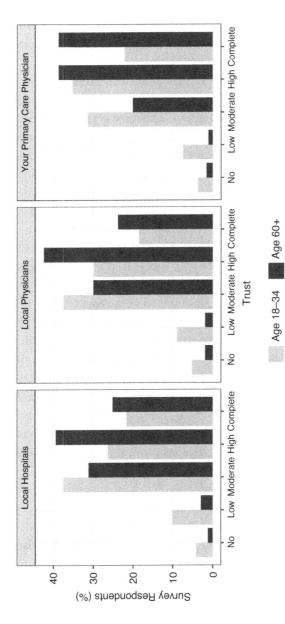

Figure 13 Reported trust in the local hospitals and physicians separated by age

respondent increased. Similarly, partisan independents were less trusting of these organizations. However, it is not clear whether the responses of the partisan independents are actually reflective of this group being younger than partisans. It is also possible that other factors create an illusion that age or partisan independents are correlated with trust in health information providers. To address this concern, this section builds a multivariate model of trust in health information providers in COVID-19.

This analysis focuses on the average of the trust assessments for all of the health information providers. The previous discussion illustrated modest differences across the various organizations, with some organizations being trusted more (e.g. the US CDC) and some less (governors), but the variation was within a narrow range. To facilitate the assessment of the multivariate model, the models take the average of trust reports for each of the actors and organizations discussed earlier in the section. The average provides a summary indicator that will provide insight into the role of multiple factors simultaneously in a multivariate model with a relatively simple linear regression.

The most important potential confounder in such a model is individual reports of concerns about COVID-19. People who are more concerned about COVID-19 may have different attitudes toward the most relevant providers of information. It may also be the case that concern about COVID-19 is related to age (due to personal vulnerability) and party identification (if the pandemic becomes politicized). To test this possibility, we compared the levels of reported concern about COVID-19 across age groups and party identification.[13]

Figure 14 illustrates the raw distribution of concern over COVID-19 in March 2020. Early in the pandemic, concern was already quite high. The modal category was "extremely" concerned. There are few respondents who are "not at all" or only "slightly" concerned. It is possible that such a strong effect creates illusory or spurious correlations between other factors (such as party identification or age).

Bivariate comparisons of expressed levels of concern about COVID-19 across age groups and party identification reveal significant differences across the groups. Figure 15 illustrates the comparison of the mean concern levels across these various groups with bars representing standard deviations. It is clear that concern increases across age groups. The concern in COVID-19 also varied across party identification with major party independents being less concerned than Republicans and Republicans being less concerned than

---

[13] The survey instrument measured concern about COVID-19 with a direct question asking whether respondents would describe their level of concern with five options: (1) "no risk at all"; (2) "slightly"; (3) "moderately"; (4) "very"; (5) "extremely."

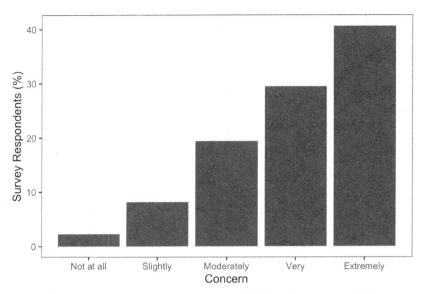

Figure 14 Reported concern about COVID-19 in March 2020

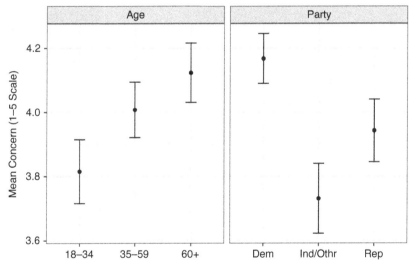

Figure 15 Reported concern about COVID-19 separated by age and political party affiliation

Democrats. This is further evidence that major party independents are not simply an intermediary category between Republicans and Democrats. Given the strong influence of pandemic concern on these key variables, we will include pandemic concern within the multivariate model. We will also include controls for race and gender. Table 8 reports the results of this multivariate regression.

Table 8 The multivariate model of the trust index for March 2020

Variable	Coefficient	Standard Error
Major Party Independents (vs. Democrats)	−.179	.052
Republicans (vs. Democrats)	.052	.051
Age 35-59 (vs. 35)	.081	.053
Age 60+ (vs. 35)	.164	.061
Black	−.040	.072
Hispanic	.020	.061
Other Race	−.046	.078
Male	.043	.043
Concern for COVID	.212	.020
Constant	2.77	.1
Observations		1,486
Adjusted R^2		.101
Residual Standard Error		.787

The multivariate model provides a clearer picture of the combination of factors influencing trust in health information providers in March 2020. As expected from the bivariate comparisons, major party independents are significantly less trusting in these agencies, with an expected trust index of .179 less than Democrats (the baseline category) Republicans are not statistically distinguishable from Democrats. Age has only a limited effect in the multivariate models, with only the oldest age category being statistically distinguishable from the youngest age cohort (the baseline category) and this statistical significance being at the .061 level. This effect, though estimated with enough uncertainty that the significance does not meet the common .05 level, is sizable with an increase of .164 to the trust index. There is reason to believe that the drop in significance for age is related to the close association of age and concern for COVID-19 creating colinearity that inflates the standard error of the related estimates.

Most interesting is the important role of pandemic concern. An increase in one step up the pandemic concern reporting options increases the expected trust index level by .214. This difference is larger than for either the oldest age category or partisan independents. Reported concern at this early stage in the pandemic seems to be a central component that differentiates those who are generally trusting of official sources of health information from those who are not.

It is important to note that these relationships are not necessarily causal. The survey technique used here does not allow for the testing of any causal relationships. While we see a strong relationship between pandemic concern and trust in health information providers, for example, we can not say which of these variables causes the other. It could be that those who were trusting became more concerned. Alternatively, it could be that the most concerned are the most attentive and developed trust in these information providers.

The relationships are clearer between age, partisan identification, and the trust index. Trust in these information providers does not age people – so the causal arrow is extremely unlikely to run from trust to age. The implausibility of the reverse causal relationship makes the claim that older people are more trusting, *ceteris paribus*, easy to interpret – though the results are weak in the multivariate model.

The connection between party identification and the trust index is more challenging to interpret. It is unlikely that trust in specific health information providers drove people out of either major political party. Party identification is generally thought of as fundamental to political attitudes – early in the funnel of causality (Campbell et al., 1960). A more specific political attitude, like trust in specific organizations or the index of trust in health information providers, is thought to be later in the causal process. This is a theoretical assertion of causality rather than empirical evidence. Stronger evidence of the connection between party identification and trust in health information providers requires data across time, whereas this data is just from March 2020.

4.4.1 Conclusions on Varieties of Trust

These results provide a more nuanced picture than often found in discussions of trust in government. First, we have found that there is a range of trust in agencies. It is not enough to assess the level of trust in "government." People report more trust in some organizations than others. The most trusted organizations or groups are the US CDC and personal physicians. These are the organization and group most likely to persuade people to adopt costly or inconvenient protective behaviors.

A more detailed multivariate model provides a clearer picture of trust in health information providers in March 2020 at the onset of the global pandemic. The strongest differences in reported trust is between people with varying levels of concern about the pandemic. The people with higher levels of concern exhibit higher levels of trust in health information providers. Major party independents are less trusting – even with these controls for demographic characteristics and concern about the pandemic. Age was also an important factor, but the estimates included enough uncertainty to render the relationship weak.

This model of trust from March 2020 is a useful starting point for an investigation. Looking at changes in trust over time may provide greater insight into the relative importance of concern, party identification, and age. Do attacks on various health information providers and the politicization of information related to the pandemic cause changes in the reported levels of trust? Does party identification become a more important predictor as the pandemic becomes caught in the partisan polarization surrounding the 2020 presidential campaign? Charting the changes in trust over time may provide more insight into how stable trust is under the pressures of the US policymaking system.

5 Dynamics of Trust

The previous discussion provided a snapshot of trust in US health agencies at the onset of the pandemic in March 2020. It was unclear how long the pandemic would last or what policies would be necessary to combat it. The months dragged on as the world continued to grapple with the nature of the pandemic and the scientific discoveries needed to combat the virus, and various efforts became entangled in partisan politics. Over this time, trust in health organizations changed as the pandemic wore on and became embroiled in US partisan politics.

Statements from President Trump provide a useful review of the timeline of the contested politics of the pandemic – and, hence, the organizations fighting the pandemic's spread.[14] The data discussed in the previous section illustrates the state of trust in US health organizations when the pandemic took root in the United States. The president was generally offering reassuring messages that the crisis would pass quickly. On March 10 (just before our survey began), President Trump told reporters at the White House, "We're prepared, and we're doing a great job with it. And it will go away. Just stay calm. It will go away." Less than a week later, President Trump announced guidelines promoting social distancing, but only for a fifteen-day period. At the same time, the president said, "With several weeks of focused effort, we can turn the corner and turn it quickly."

By the end of the month, the president's statements began to reflect the controversy over efforts to combat the spread of the pandemic. The president often repeated the phrase "we cannot let the cure be worse than the problem itself" (tweeted on March 22 in all capital letters).

One can understand how many people were confused when April came and there was no end in sight for the pandemic. If anything, the expected end

---

[14] Statements by President Trump referenced in this section are quoted from www.factcheck.org/ 2020/10/timeline-of-trumps-covid-19-comments/.

seemed farther and farther away with each passing day. On April 2, the president stated during a task force briefing that "[t]he sacrifices we make over the next four weeks will have countless American lives saved." In a task force briefing just two days later, the president continued, "This will be probably the toughest week, between this week and next week. And there'll be a lot of death, unfortunately, but a lot less death than if this wasn't done."

Notice that the time frame has shifted but was still being counted in a small number of weeks. People may have reasonably interpreted this to mean that the well-informed president believed the pandemic would be over in April. That vision would darken through the weeks of April and into May. Conflict emerged, between the president and various US state governors and with international organizations. On April 13, the president stated (again at a task force briefing):

> I'm going to put it very simply: The president of the United States has the authority to do what the president has the authority to do, which is very powerful. The president of the United States calls the shots.

The next day he announced:

> Today I am instructing my administration to halt funding of the World Health Organization while a review is conducted to assess [its] role in severely mismanaging and covering up the spread of the coronavirus.

The tenor of statements related to the pandemic changed in April. It became clear that steps to limit the spread of the pandemic would become controversial and pulled into partisan debates. The pandemic was now thoroughly politicized. This culminated in the president tweeting "LIBERATE MICHIGAN" (capitalization in the original). The president was now publicly opposed to efforts in some (Democrat-controlled) states ranging from mask mandates to business closings. The pandemic was the most prominent topic, but it was now pulled into partisan conflicts – a process that would continue through the year.

This section will explore how trust in health organizations evolved through this process of politicization and the growing sense that the pandemic would take many months – maybe years – to address. Most research in trust in government has used annual data to assess the changes in trust over time. This level of precision has revealed the connection between party identification, economic factors, and trust. However, there is little known about the dynamics of trust in administrative agencies over shorter periods of time. How quickly do levels of trust adjust to new circumstances? Do these adjustments vary by organization? This section will explore these questions.

5.1 The Evolution of Trust in US Health Organizations

The natural starting place is to wonder why we would expect trust to change at all. The previous section demonstrated that trust was closely related to age category and party identification – two slow-changing characteristics. Based on this alone, we might not expect to see much change at all. Changes in party identification are rare, and not many people will be changing age category during 2020.

Looking back at the more basic theory of trust offered by Coleman (1994), there is reason to expect that there may be changes despite these associations. The willingness to trust is a function of the potential consequences (and their probabilities) of accepting the advice of the advice giver (in the case of trust in information). The perceived consequences of COVID-19 and the policies intended to combat the spread of the pandemic were very much changing through 2020. As one perceives increased costs of pandemic measures (all else being equal), one is less likely to simply accept the advice of information providers – that is, one is less likely to act based on simple trust in the information providers. While the slow-changing nature of age and party identification creates limits on how much change we are likely to see, the changes in perceived costs of policies and risks of COVID-19 may drive changes in trust in health information providers.

These competing factors (factors promoting stasis and factors promoting change) interact in a relatively predictable way. The factors promoting stasis (the significant correlations between party identification, age, and trust) will put downward pressure on large increases in trust and upward pressure against large decreases in trust. Only in a region around the starting level of trust would we expect to see changes – mirroring changes in concern about COVID-19.

If there were little change in reported concern of COVID-19, we would expect very little change in trust assessments. Large changes in concern, however, could trigger changes in trust through the balance of risks represented by trusting health information related to COVID-19. The progress of average concern in COVID-19 from March through the rest of 2020 is reported on Figure 16.[15] This figure reveals that concern for COVID-19 was highest at the start of April (4.3 out of 5) but decayed through mid-May to a dynamic equilibrium around 3.7 (the shades represent 95 percent confidence on this and

---

[15] The survey months do not correspond exactly to calendar month. Except for the first wave, the waves all included between twenty-eight and twenty-nine days and are assigned numbers based on the sequence of these twenty-eight- to twenty-nine-day windows. Only the last wave (wave 10) includes as many days of the previous month (November) as the tenth month following March (December).

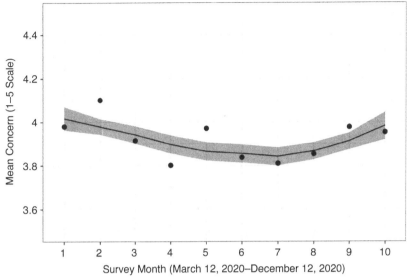

Figure 16 The evolution of concern in COVID-19 from March 2020 to December 2020

all following figures). This decay creates a "flattened U" share of relatively rapid decline followed by a new steady level.

If changes in concern over COVID-19 are a primary driver of average trust in health organizations, we would expect to see a "flattened U" shape – as opposed to steady levels across the period reflecting the low levels of change in party identification and age group. The "flattened U" may be attenuated from above and below as party identification and age group pressure trust levels to remain the same despite changes in other elements of the trust decision.

The "flattened U" shape is what we see in the changes in average trust in health information providers throughout 2020. Figure 17 illustrates the time series. It is worth remembering that this average includes the ratings of seven agencies on a five-point scale. This average was at a high level in the first two months and then dropped in April and May to a new equilibrium level. The only deviation from the "flattened U" pattern is the lack of evidence of an increase in trust in the last couple months – resulting in a shape more like a "lazy J."

As the previous section detailed, there is considerable variation in the trust ratings of specific health organizations. The US CDC had the highest ratings while state governors had the lowest ratings in March 2020 within the set analyzed. Not all organizations may have experienced the same "lazy J" evolutionary pattern (or the "flattened U" of concern for COVID-19). Some organizations may have experienced more or less change over time.

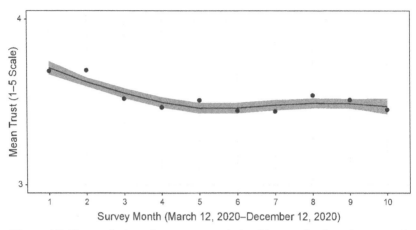

Figure 17 The evolution of average trust in health organizations from March 2020 to December 2020

We observed three general sets of organizations based on the March surveys. The top-rated organizations were either specialized federal units (the US CDC and the US HHS) or specialized local units (local hospitals and local physicians). The state governors were somewhat local (compared to the federal agencies) but not specialized in health. The state health agencies are specialized in health but more distant than local sources of information.

The susceptibility of organizations to changes in trust may be driven by various factors. The section opened with a discussion of the increasing politicization of the pandemic. If this politicization reduces trust, it will more dramatically affect distant (federal) and non-expert (governors) information providers. Figure 18 illustrates that these expectations roughly hold.

A first look at Figure 18 shows that the "Lazy J" pattern among the average trust ratings does conceal variation in dynamics through the year. The four state and federal health information providers experienced a noticeable decline in trust through the year. The federal agencies (US CDC and US HHS) have something like the "lazy J" pattern observed in the overall average. These organization had high ratings early in the period (March and April), but this value declined rapidly after the high starting point. If anything, it looks like the highly rated federal agencies lost a relatively large amount of trust because they had more room to fall.

The state-level agencies experienced similar levels of losses of trust as the federal agencies, but there is reason to believe that state agencies have not found a new equilibrium. While the federal agencies had settled into a new trust level by late summer (and even may be regaining some of that trust), the state agencies have seen two periods of decline. The second period of decline still seems to be underway in December 2020.

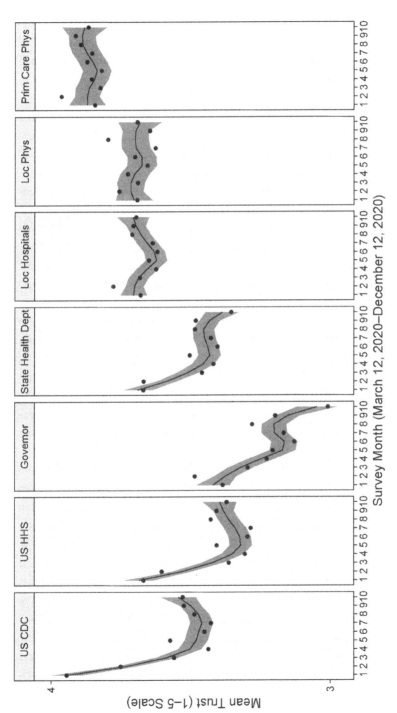

Figure 18 The evolution of trust in each health organization from March 2020 to December 2020

The local organizations exhibit much more durability. They do not seem to have been caught in the same cycle of decline – possibly related to the politicization – of the federal and state organizations. The local organizations all stayed relatively stable through the sampling period. These organizations had levels of trust in December 2020 that were quite similar to those reported in March 2020. At most, there was a small drop in the summer, but this is within a narrow band of variation. The pattern resembles an attenuated version of the "flattened U" seen in the time path of concern for COVID-19. The consistency of this pattern may suggest a strongly protective influence of low social distance attributed to local health organizations.

Figure 18 reveals three types of trajectories for trust ratings. The expert federal agencies experience an early drop followed by a new equilibrium level mirroring the "Lazy J" pattern in the overall average. The state agencies, however, do not stop with the initial drop experienced by the federal agencies. They experience a second drop that may be continuing through the end of 2020. The state group includes both an expert organization (state health departments) and a generalist organization (governors) – but both experienced the double dip. This seems to indicate that state health agencies experience patterns in losses of trust that are more similar to the generalist state counterpart than the federal specialist counterparts.

The local organizations stand alone having weathered the tumultuous early period that cost the federal agencies and avoided the double dip experienced by the state agencies. Respondents gave similar ratings to their local health organizations through the period despite the controversies and uncertainties present throughout 2020.

The advantage of local health organizations may be quite useful for health communicators. The resilience of the local health organizations makes them an ideal partner to provide information. People are more trusting of information from these actors and may be more likely to take up this advice – especially when policies rely on voluntary compliance in the absence of enforcement. In such an environment, the best division of labor may be for specialist organizations to develop information and local providers to disseminate that information – with state organizations providing support rather than seeking to be the attributed provider of the information.

The evolutionary patterns reported in Figure 18 show that there is variability based on agency. However, these patterns only reflect the average trust in these organizations. As the previous section revealed, this average may conceal variations in trust among different groups within the sample. That section revealed, for example, that there were significant differences in trust levels between partisan independents and partisans (both Democrats and Republicans). The trust trajectories may also vary across different social groups. Sections 5.2 and 5.3 will report on the trust trajectories for specific social groups – age group and party identification.

5.2 Age Differences in the Evolution of Trust

The average change in trust over time concealed interesting variation across agencies with three distinct trajectories – "lazy J" (the US CDC and the HHS), "double dip" (state health agencies and state governors), and steady across the year with a minor dip in the middle (a "flattened U" for local organizations). This section will explore whether there are more differences across the age groups within our sample. In the previous section, there was evidence that older respondents were more trusting than others in March 2020 (more or less across the organizations). This section will explore whether the higher trust levels persist for older respondents or whether this population experiences different trajectories of trust. The observed trajectories of trust in specific organizations appear in Figure 19.

The starting point is the federal agencies. For the two federal agencies (the US CDC and the HHS), the pattern of the older and younger age groups is similar – but not identical. Figure 20 zooms in for a more detailed view of these two organizations, trust trajectories.

The two groups have roughly the same trust trajectories through 2020. In the earliest period, older respondents were slightly more trusting of federal health agencies. The early advantage went away – first for the US HHS. Once the older group merges with the younger group, they do not separate again, aside from a small period in mid-summer wherein older respondents had lower trust ratings than their younger counterparts.

The older group is one with greater concern over COVID-19, and that may explain the small differences here. Concern was at its highest level when the older age group had the higher levels of trust. The drop in concern by the early summer roughly coincides with the drop in trust for the older age cohort – resulting in the mitigation of age as a distinctive influence on trust.

The trajectory for state health organizations appears in Figure 21. The double-dip trajectory is preserved in the age group comparison plot. For all four groups (two age groups across two state organizations), there is a noticeable double dip. There was an initial decline from March through early summer (similar to the trajectories for federal health organizations). However, the state organizations saw a second decline beginning around October – just as the federal election was imminent. Again, the older respondents were more trusting than their younger counterparts, but this difference decayed as the months

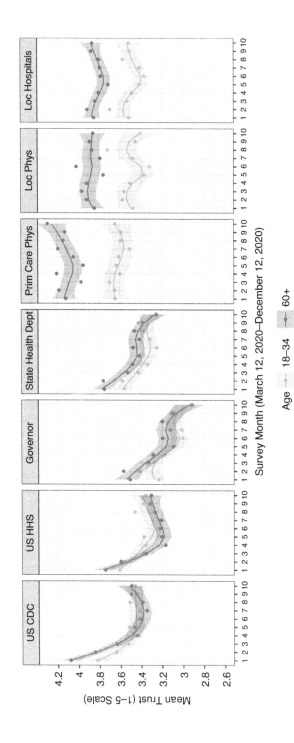

Figure 19 The evolution of trust in each health organization separated by age group from March 2020 to December 2020

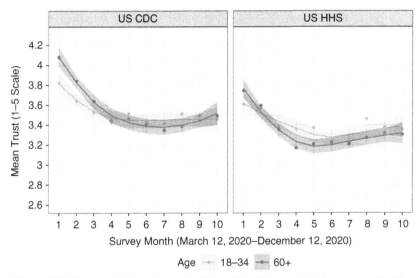

Figure 20 The evolution of trust in federal health organizations separated by age group from March 2020 to December 2020

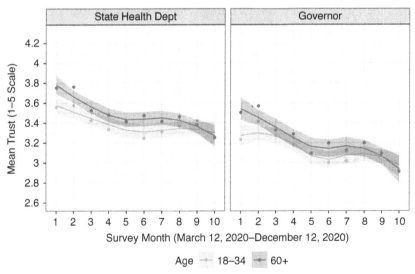

Figure 21 The evolution of trust in state health organizations separated by age group from March 2020 to December 2020

wore on. For state health departments, the older age group was noticeably more trusting until after the federal election. With the state governors, however, the older group converged with the younger group sooner, with significant overlap in the confidence intervals by early summer. The double-dip trajectory is the same across both groups, but, like with the federal agencies, the difference

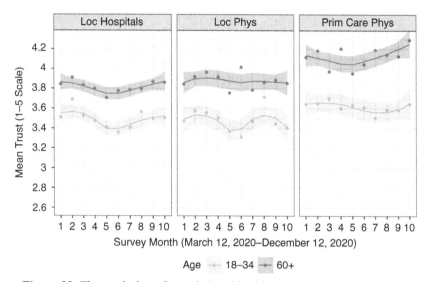

Figure 22 The evolution of trust in local health organizations separated by age group from March 2020 to December 2020

between the age groups decays through the year until the two groups are indistinguishable in their levels of trust.

The final set of organizations, the local organizations, are represented in Figure 22. Here the age groups are quite distinct. The higher levels of trust observed in March among the older age group persist through the year for all three local organizations. There is what may be a dip in the middle for local hospitals and physicians, but this dip is minor. Hospitals and local physicians weathered the year well. Primary care physicians (including "your" physician) exhibited a different path, with the higher levels of trust observed in the older age group, but in this case there is early evidence of increases in trust late in the year for both age groups. The increase seems to have started earlier and been larger in the older age group.

Overall, the patterns, for difference in age suggest that there were changes over time but that these changes were largely parallel across our two age groups. There was a period of convergence of the group for the federal and state organizations, with the older respondents beginning to more closely resemble their younger counterparts. For local organizations, older respondents did not converge but instead preserved the greater levels of trust observed in the earliest period for the older age group.

5.3 Partisan Differences in the Evolution of Trust

The previous section argued that differences between major party partisans and major party independents were significant at the start of the pandemic in March.

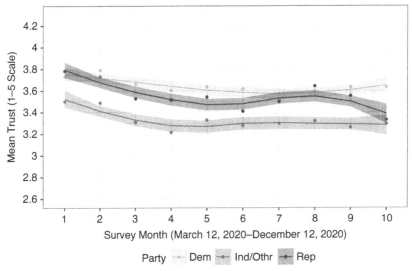

Figure 23 The evolution of the trust index separated by party identification from March 2020 to December 2020

The overall index suggests that there was a "shallow U"-shaped evolution of trust through the year. Given the importance of party identification early in the year and the ample evidence of politicization of health information, it is important to assess whether the trajectory of trust through the year was the same across members of different political parties (here comparing Democrats, Republicans, and major party independents).[16]

Figure 23 compares the trajectory of trust assessments through 2020 separated by party identification. The snapshot of March was a peculiar point in time compared to the rest of the year. Republicans and Democrats had similar trust assessments, whereas party independents had significantly lower trust ratings. The trajectory for Democrats is relatively simple. They started at nearly the highest level of trust (Republicans were slightly higher, but the difference was statistically indistinguishable). Democrats soon became the most trusting group and retained that title throughout the pandemic – with Republicans quickly declining in trust and never getting back to the same levels as Democrats except for a brief dalliance with the same level of trust as the Democrats in the period immediately preceding the election (around October). The Democrats ended the year with significantly higher levels of trust than the Republicans or the party independents.

---

[16] It is important to recall that the major party independents category includes those who identify with no party or who only identify with a minor party like the Green Party or the Libertarian Party.

The major party independents have a similarly simple trajectory. They began March with significantly lower levels of trust than the party members (both Democrats and Republicans). They lost trust from April through May until settling into a new equilibrium that persisted through the end of the year. They created a lower boundary for trust just as the Democrats defined an upper boundary.

The trajectory for the Republican respondents is more complex. There is a danger in over-interpreting small changes in the time series given the large amount of data (even small changes can be statistically significant with large samples). Taking the trajectory of the Republicans at face value, their levels of trust dropped parallel to the party independents' through the early summer. This was a period in which the Republican respondents began to converge toward party independents, but they plateaued in the summer before experiencing an increase through the month preceding the federal election. Soon after the election, the decline began again as Republicans converged with major party independents at the floor of the trust ratings. This changing trajectory reflects the tension between their party leadership both running the federal organizations (which may increase trust) and questioning the appropriateness of state and local restrictions to combat the spread of the pandemic. It may not be a surprise that under such conditions we observe a sinusoidal pattern for Republican trust in health organizations.

The confusing trajectory of the Republicans may become clearer as we break the index down to look at the trajectories for specific organizations.

Figure 24 illustrates the trajectories for each organization separated by partisan identification. The general patterns look similar – with some separate dynamics related to different party identifications. More detailed images of the trajectories for federal organizations appear in Figure 25.

A focus on federal agencies provides a clearer view of the role of party identification in shaping the trajectory of trust. The case of the US CDC provides a fairly clear narrative. The Republicans started with trusting the US CDC at a slightly higher level than Democrats (slightly - but not in a statistically significant manner) in March. This level of trust dropped quickly, though. By April, Republicans had significantly lower levels of trust in the US CDC than Democrats but greater than major partisan independents. By May, the Republican respondents had levels of trust similar to major party independents. There was a brief period around September when the Republicans became more trusting of the US CDC than partisan independents (but still lower than Democrats). It is important to note that this is a year in which the Republicans controlled the US presidency and the Senate. Traditional wisdom related to trust in government (in general) is that respondents who share partisanship with

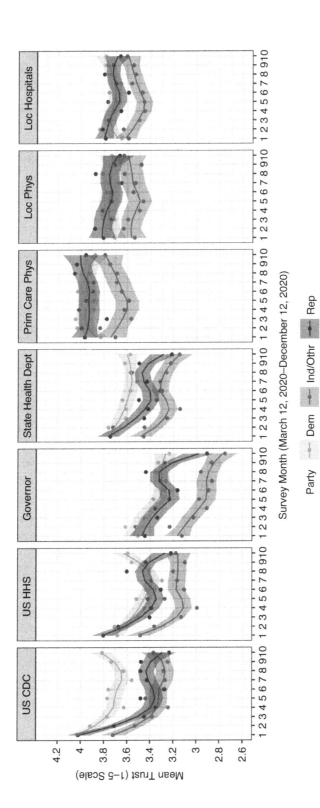

Figure 24 The evolution of trust in each health organization separated by party identification from March 2020 to December 2020

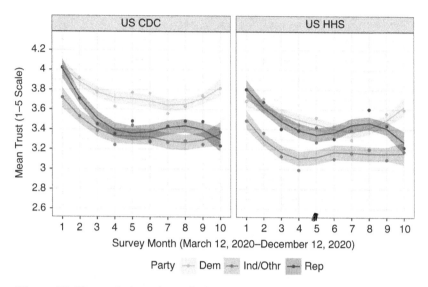

Figure 25 The evolution of trust in federal health organizations separated by party identification from March 2020 to December 2020

the president are expected to be more trusted. The trajectory of trust in the case of Republicans and the US CDC suggests that the most trusting audience for some agencies may be out-party members with affinities for a specific policy area.

It is important to note from Figure 25 that the Democrats did report less trust in the US CDC after March. Like Republicans and major party independents, Democrats reported declining levels of trust from April through June. The decline was smaller than for the other groups, and a new equilibrium emerged in summer. There was even some evidence of an increase in trust following the elections (in November and December). Overall, the trajectory for Democrats looks like a slightly exaggerated version of the overall trust index at slightly higher average levels.

Major party independents exhibit a pattern similar to the Democrats (and the overall trust index) but at a lower level. They started at lower levels of trust than partisans but still experienced declines through June. At that point they leveled out at a low level. By the end of the year, their trajectory had merged with the Republicans – even with a slight uptick at the end of year, though the difference between Republicans and major party independents was not statistically distinguishable at that point.

The pattern for state-level agencies is quite different, as illustrated in Figure 26. The trust in state health departments sees a mixture of patterns, with the Democrats reporting a slow decay in trust before a stabilization in

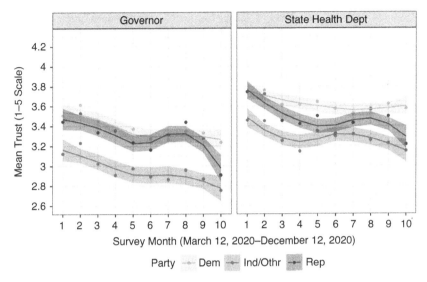

Figure 26 The evolution of trust in state health organizations separated by party identification from March 2020 to December 2020

September and major party independents seeing an early decline (from April through June) followed by a brief and small increase for the rest of the summer followed finally by another slow decline from September through December. The Republicans bounce between these two groups, with a similar pattern to that of the partisan independents but at a slightly higher level of trust and a slight delay in the increase and final decline.

When we substitute the party match assessment for the party identification assessment, a similar story emerges. Figure 27 illustrates the pattern. The co-partisans are more trusting - as one would expect. However, the pattern of variations for the out-party respondents resembles that of Republicans over-all, with a rapid loss followed by an increase around September and another drop at the very end of the year. The drop is much more pronounced for the governor than for the state health agencies – possibly reflecting an expertise effect buffering the agency that does not protect the generalist governors. This also represents suggestive evidence of a politicization of these institutions as trust of non-co-partisan state officials varied through the year with an overall decline. Further work on whether different partisan identifiers report different levels of trust as non-co-partisans is warranted.

The trajectories for local health organizations are quite similar to those of the trust index, as illustrated in Figure 28. With local health organizations, the Democrats and Republicans have similar trust ratings, and these ratings change little through the year. The local health organizations seem to have been

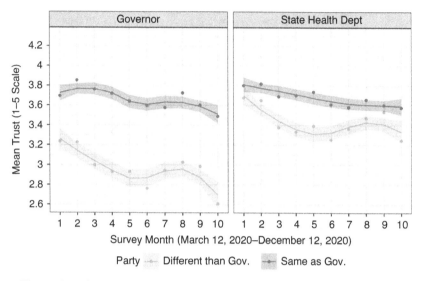

Figure 27 The evolution of trust in state health organizations separated by party match from March 2020 to December 2020

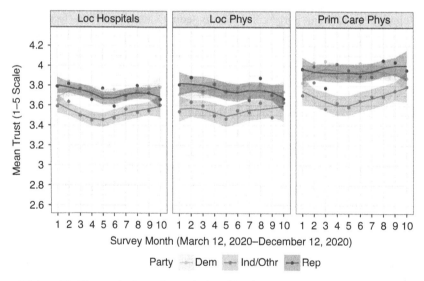

Figure 28 The evolution of trust in local health organizations separated by party identification from March 2020 to December 2020

buffered from the polarization that saw Republican levels of trust drop farther, faster than the Democrats, – most noticeably contrasting with federal health organizations. The major party independents have lower trust levels throughout the year, though these trust levels are fairly stable. There is evidence of convergence of the three groups – particularly in the case of primary care physicians – in the final month of the year.

Together, the trajectories of trust separated by party identification provides some hints as to the nature of the changes in trust over time and the nature of party polarization. Local organizations experienced very little decay in trust over the year (though there were differences between the political parties as to the starting levels). It is the more distant organizations from most respondents – the state and federal agencies – where the most decay is seen, with the greater differences across political parties. The Republicans saw greater declines than those seen in other groups – one expression of partisan polarization. While trust in health agencies in March was remarkably similar between the Democrats and Republicans, Republicans saw much greater volatility through the year. The polarization seen in this case involves a greater reaction of the Republican respondents rather than a dramatic change. Polarization in 2020 was gradual and inconsistent across time. However, these dynamics illustrate that changes in trust are possible on a short time scale in reaction to new information and that these changes may persist for months.

5.4 A Multivariate Model of the Dynamics of Trust in Health Organizations

As with Section 4, the simple visual comparisons can be misleading because they are essentially bivariate. In this case, the figures compare trust across time and across age or party identification. However, other variables may also be important – most notably, concern of COVID-19. This section will present a broader multivariate model of trust across time. Specifically, it will provide tests of whether key variables mattered over the entire year and whether we saw a general drop in trust as seemed to be the case with the simple trajectory of the trust index.

There is reason to believe that the changes in the trajectory of trust in health organizations is not an artifact of changes in other variables (with one exception). The demographic variables included in the model (age, race, ethnicity, and gender) are slowly changing characteristics that are unlikely to change enough from month to month to explain a change in the trust index within a single year. However, including these variables in the multivariate model is helpful to reduce the influence of any potential imbalance between months because differences in sampling for these variables will be mitigated by inclusion in the final model.

The variable most likely to change over the year – and most likely to confound the comparisons presented earlier in the section – is concern for

Table 9 The multivariate model of the trust index for 2020 with month fixed-effects

Variable	Coefficient	Standard Error
Major Party Independents (vs. Democrats)	−.209	.020
Republicans (vs. Democrats)	−.006	.020
Age 35–59 (vs. 18–35)	.092	.019
Age 60+ (vs. 18–35)	.107	.022
Black	−.173	.026
Hispanic	−.029	.022
Other Race	−.066	.030
Male	.125	.016
Concern for COVID-19	.225	.007
April	−.022	.033
May	−.149	.033
June	−.176	.033
July	−.157	.033
August	−.197	.033
September	−.196	.033
October	−.119	.033
November	−.171	.033
December	−.223	.033
Constant	2.75	.041
Observations		10,347
Adjusted R^2		.132
Residual Standard Error		.793

COVID-19. This is an attitude that is more likely to change from month to month and may exert a strong influence on the trajectory of the trust index. It could be that the trajectories observed for party identification and age are artifacts of the differences in concern for COVID-19 among these groups. A multivariate test helps address this potentially confounding effect.

Table 9 presents the results of a linear regression model of the trust index pooling the data from March 2020 to December 2020. This model includes the same variables as the multivariate model from March but adds in fixed effects for each month to better track whether there were trends from month to month – even when controlling for key factors like party identification, age, and concern for COVID-19. We also included gender and race as control variables.

The multivariate model reinforces, rather than contradicts, the previous discussion of the influence of age and party identification. Across the entire year, major party independents have significantly lower levels of expected trust (.2 points in average trust). The oldest age group, similarly, has an expected trust level that is .1 points higher than of the youngest age group. These values are the average effects across the entire year, but that reinforces the importance of these variables across the year.

The estimate for the difference between Democrats and Republicans is small and not statistically significant. This is not entirely unexpected given the figures that illustrated how Republicans bounced throughout the year from resembling Democrats and major party independents. The average coefficient for Republicans ends up indistinguishable, there being no difference between Democrats and Republicans.

The strongest effect is still concern for COVID-19. A one-unit increase in concern for COVID-19 is associated with a .23 increase in the expected level of trust across the year. This coefficient is the largest in the model, narrowly exceeding the influence of reporting that one is a partisan independent.

Figure 29 presents an alternative method for visualizing the comparison of these influences – including the month fixed effects. The array of month fixed effects illustrates that the general trajectory of trust reported in Figure 17 holds even when controlling for the various variables included in the multivariate model.

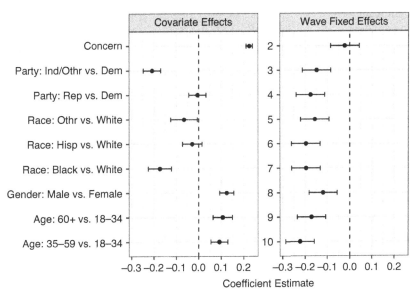

Figure 29 Coefficient plot for the multivariate fixed-effects model of the trust index from March 2020 to December 2020

Figure 29 provides a visualization of how strong and stable the relationship between concern for COVID-19 and the trust index is through the year – as well as the negative relationship between major party independents and trust in health organizations. There are also stable effects related to Black respondents and male respondents (though those are not topics we explore in detail here).

It is the month fixed effects that tell the most interesting story from the multivariate model. Each month fixed effect represents the average difference in trust ratings (controlling for all of the other variables). The baseline for the fixed effect comparisons is March. So, the wave 2 fixed effect represents surveys completed in the second wave (approximately April 2020) while wave 10 represents the average differences in trust at the end of the year (November/December 2020). After the initial surveys in March, the reported average levels of trust in health organizations stayed relatively stable for April (the drop is not statistically significant) before dropping in May. The new low levels of trust are sustained through the year with only minor changes that are not statistically significant. The uptick in October, for example, is not statistically significant and is reversed in wave 9 (mostly November 2020).

The series of month fixed effects confirm that the overall trajectory reported earlier in the section is not an artifact of changes in the other variables – such as potential changes in concern over COVID-19. Slight variations observable in the time series are not statistically significant (after the drop around May), but evidence of any changes beyond that are artifactual and not statistically significant.

The multivariate model assesses whether the average level of trust changes through the year while assuming constant relationships between the other independent variables and average trust in health organizations. This model does not provide evidence related to whether the the relationship between independent variables (say, concern for COVID-19) and average trust changed throughout the year. To better assess the stability of the independent variables over time, Figure 30 compares the coefficient for the same model estimates in March to one estimated in December.

The comparison of the March and the wave 10 sub-samples provides a useful view of what changed throughout the year. The relationship between concern for COVID-19 and average trust in health organizations is statistically indistinguishable between these two sub-samples. Similarly, the negative influence of major party independence on trust is not statistically significant. However, the influence of Republican party affiliation changes through the year. In March, there is a positive influence (though the statistical significance is marginal). By December, Republicans were significantly less trusting (both in terms of statistical significance and substantive significance). This comparison provides a

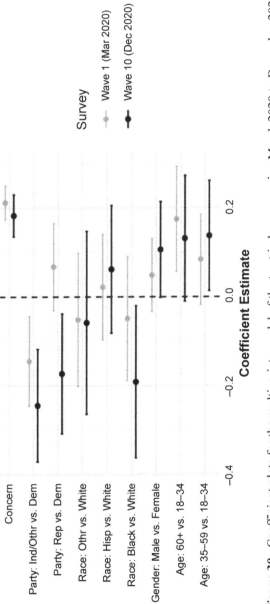

Figure 30 Coefficient plots for the multivariate model of the trust index comparing March 2020 to December 2020

more formal assessment of the dynamics of trust in health organizations over the year. Many of the drivers of trust were stable in their influence, but some – most notably Republican affiliation – changed dramatically through the year.

5.5 Conclusion

Together, these results provide a picture of the evolution of trust in health organizations from the start of the pandemic in March 2020 through the end of the year. Trust declined sharply early into the pandemic and stayed at these lower levels through a variety of major developments, including the recognition that the pandemic would last months (or years) rather than weeks, political controversies related to the pandemic, and the approval of a safe and effective vaccine.

A key question is the extent to which one can call these developments politicization or polarization. The evidence here is not clear in regards to these labels – in part because the labels themselves are unclear. There is evidence here consistent with the argument that Republicans became more skeptical (taking that as the opposite of trusting) of health organizations. Republicans moved from trusting these health organizations at approximately the same level as Democrats in March to (following a somewhat circuitous path) ending up closer to partisan independents by December.

It is also important not to overstate these changes. One reading media coverage or social media may have the impression that Republicans have changed from trusting to untrusting. This is an exaggeration. Republicans have lost about .3 points of trust on a five-point scale. This is statistically significant but is an effect size on the order of a one-point change in concern about COVID-19. Republicans did not move from the top of the scale to the bottom (which would be a four-point swing) but experienced a much more modest change.

Another useful comparison is that the the general drop in trust from March to December (the average loss across all respondents, controlling for concern about COVID-19, party identification, etc.) is larger than the difference between the change experienced by Republicans in that same time period (but approximately the same size). Republican levels of trust dropped more than Democrats' did, but only on approximately the same scale as Democrats experienced relative to their own reports in this time – as a result, Republicans experienced approximately twice the drop in trust through the year.

The most important lesson from the analysis is how much dynamism there is within the year. Most trust research measures trust on an annual basis. The data here illustrate that there are interesting dynamics from month to month. This is not to say that there are not many lessons one can draw from annual measurement of trust (or, even, cross-sectional measurement of trust) in government and its units. Rather, there are new avenues to explore by considering shorter periods of time than a year.

6 Conclusions and Future Directions

As the United States continues to grapple with the COVID-19 pandemic, protective information has become of vital importance. The public struggles to figure out what is safe to do, how to reduce their own risks, and how long the crisis is likely to last. The crisis is of such broad consequence that the public turns to organizations with broad responsibilities and broad expertise – public organizations. Our question is whether the public trusts these public organizations (federal, state, and local).

Our survey of the American public suggests that there is a surprising amount of trust in these organizations – though the trust varies. The most trusted organizations are those that are the most specialized and expert (the US CDC) and the most local (personal physicians). This overall trend, though, conceals important variation. Trust varies within the public as well as across the organizations. Admittedly few people report the lowest levels of trust in any of the organizations. However, some groups report more of the lowest levels of trust – notably major party independents, with their low trust in all of the organizations in our analysis.

Possibly the most interesting patterns emerging from these early comparisons of trust across different social groups regard major party independents. It is not the case that Democrats or Republicans are uniformly more or less trusting in relevant actors and organizations. In many cases, these two groups were equally trusting. In some cases, especially regarding the local actors and organizations, the Republicans were more trusting than Democrats. What stands out, though, is the patterns for major party independents. Major party independents are less trusting of our set of organizations across the board (barring a single comparison where the distinction is not statistically significant). It is clear, then, that major party independents are not a middle category between Democrats and Republicans. They represent a distinctive category – possibly rejecting the party system entirely, based on their lack of trust in social institutions. This suggests that comparisons of Democrats and Republicans on issues such as personal protective actions and support for policies combating the spread of the pandemic may be less important than comparisons of these two groups to self-described major party independents. Of course, future work will need to better characterize how coherent a group major party independents are using more targeted research designs.

Viewing the development of trust across time reinforces some of the most important lessons. All groups experience a drop in trust after the initial period (in April or May). Major party independents experience such a drop and retain their position as the least trusting group. Through the year, Republicans vacillate between having similar ratings as Democrats and having similar ratings of major party independents.

The time path of trust in these health organizations suggests that a period of remarkable success for health research ran parallel to a broad drop in trust in the information coming from the most prestigious health organizations. Considered by many to be outside of politics, even organizations like the US CDC saw a decrease in trust as the country integrated COVID-19 efforts into its political arguments (which only served to heat up as the US federal elections neared in November).

The development of trust through the year also cuts against some of the stronger language related to the political polarization of the US electorate as the election approached. There was considerable concern that polarization of the public would lead to half of the country not taking simple protective actions (e.g. mask wearing) as that group had lost trust in key health organizations. This fear was not without grounding but overstated. There was a loss of trust in the US CDC, to take a prominent example, among Republicans, but this drop was not from fully trusting to fully distrusting. Instead, the drops are adjustments within a point (or category) of trust. Factors like concern about COVID-19 are just as important as partisan identification.

The connection between party identification and COVID-19 points to an important limitation of this study. While this study does include data across time, it is not a panel study with the same respondents across the year. A change over time does not reflect a specific series of changes in respondents monitored across time. Instead, the survey includes separate samples for each month. This means that the analysis cannot trace changes within a respondent (e.g. changes in their concern over COVID-19 or changes in their party identification). This research design compares sampled populations at each point in time.

The pooled time-series approach makes it impossible to render strong causal claims about the patterns reported in this Element. There are no measurements of the same person in consecutive points in time. So, we do not observe changes in party identification or concern about COVID-19. The data only reveal patterns across the samples. A panel design would be necessary to assess whether a change in a given person's concern in COVID-19 led to changes in party identification (including an abandonment of a party identification) or changing reports of trust in health organizations. These data reveal patterns in group averages – but firm conclusions about individual changes would require a different research design.

6.1 A Road Forward for Public Administration?

This snapshot contributes to a broader discussion within the field of public administration. As discussed at the start of the Element, we face what seems to be a crisis in confidence in government (Kettl, 2019). Some of the data presented here undercut the argument (only slightly). While there was variation, there were many actors and organizations held in high esteem by a vast majority of Americans – notably the US CDC and personal physicians. If there is a general crisis in trust in government, it is not in evidence for the US CDC and, to a lesser extent, other organizations and actors, with a notable exception. The lowest-rated actors, were the state governors. These are the only elected actors in our set (not counting the choice of a personal physician as elected), and yet they have the lowest evaluations among their own voters. Especially the more expert organizations, like the US CDC, were trusted, and that trust translated into increased intentions to take protective actions and support more general policies. The crisis in trust in government, which we believe is a real problem for the field of public administration, was not evident in this particular grouping of actors and organizations – though these organizations may be outliers due to their expertise and the salience of that expertise to an emerging crisis.

Two patterns seems to compete within our data to explain the relatively high ratings of organizations within our study compared to the general sense of crisis. Expert organizations, as mentioned, seem to defy the sense of a distrusted government. Moreover, though, the local organizations did well, with particular advantage held by personal physicians. This pattern supports the general notion that people trust others more when they work with those organizations and see how they share their values. This is more likely with local organizations than with distant federal bureaucracies. In addition to building the perception of expertise,[17] building trust in government organizations may need to start close to home. It may not be a polished ad campaign for federal agencies that matters most. It may be the programs that bring residents into their city governments and local agencies to see how civil servants are just like them and share their values. Trust in government may need to be grown at the local level and flow upward – despite our disciplinary tradition of disproportionately focusing on federal agencies and their management.

---

[17] One can find in the history of the FDA a superb example of an organization that built a reputation for expertise – and the challenges they faced still (Carpenter, 2014).

If we think the first future direction is how to build trust, the second is how best to use trust. How can trusted organizations best communicate important risk assessment and protective action information so as to maximize compliance with recommended protective actions? It is clear from the data reported here that some agencies are well-regarded and that this regard is likely related to compliance with recommended protective actions (Robinson et al., 2020). How can agencies best leverage their reputations to ensure they wring every bit of potential protection out of their reputation? This is a question that will require a different set of research tools to assess effective branding strategies for well-regarded organizations. Public administration scholars may need to turn to literature in private-sector business management for inspiration.

As we proceed through the COVID-19 crisis, it is clear that answers to these questions will be of vital importance. More than a year after the crisis began, there is considerable medical uncertainty about the nature of the disease. Early efforts to limit exposure to contaminated surfaces have given way to a focus on preventing the spread of airborne particles. Vaccine research continues alongside early efforts to distribute vaccines to the most vulnerable populations. Mixed evidence suggests that the virus itself may suppress immune response in a way that makes our traditional approach to vaccination unlikely to achieve any version of herd immunity. On a more grounded front, people wonder what (if any) forms of travel and vacations are relatively safe. People still hunger for information. It will fall to public organizations and their partners to provide the best information available so that the public can protect themselves and support policies that will make everyone safer.

References

Arnold, Peri E. 1998. *Making the Managerial Tendency*. Lawrence: University of Kansas Press.

Banda, Kevin K., and Justin H. Kirkland. 2018. "Legislative party polarization and trust in state legislatures." *American Politics Research* 46(4):596–628.

Berrens, Robert P., Alok K. Bohara, Hank Jenkins-Smith, Carol Silva, and David L. Weimer. 2003. "The advent of Internet surveys for political research: A comparison of telephone and Internet samples." *Political Analysis* 11(1):1–22. http://pan.oxfordjournals.org/content/11/1/1.short.

Campbell, Angus, Philip E. Converse, Warren E. Miller, and Donald E. Stokes. 1960. *The American Voter*. Chicago, IL: University of Chicago Press.

Carpenter, Daniel. 2014. *Reputation and Power: Organizational Image and Pharmaceutical Regulation at the FDA*. Princeton, NJ: Princeton University Press.

Carpenter, Daniel. 2019. "La réputation organisationnelle de l'état fédéral dans un contexte général de malaise politique." *Revue francaise d'administration publique* 170(2):385–396.

Chanley, Virginia A., Thomas J. Rudolph, and Wendy M. Rahn. 2000. "The origins and consequences of public trust in government: A time series analysis." *Public Opinion Quarterly* 64(3):239–256.

Citrin, Jack. 1974a. "Comment: The political relevance of trust in government." *American Political Science Review* 68(3):973–988.

Coleman, James S. 1994. *Foundations of Social Theory*. Cambridge, MA: Belknap Press.

Easton, David. 1953. *The Political System: An Inquiry into the State of Political Science*. New York: Knopf.

Eiser, J. Richard, Tom Stafford, John Henneberry, and Philip Catney. 2009. "'Trust me, I'm a scientist (not a developer)': Perceived expertise and motives as predictors of trust in assessment of risk from contaminated land." *Risk Analysis: An International Journal* 29(2):288–297.

Fukuyama, Francis. 1996. *Trust: Human Nature and the Reconstitution of Social Order*. New York: Simon and Schuster.

Gershtenson, Joseph, Jeffrey Ladewig, and Dennis L. Plane. 2006. "Parties, institutional control, and trust in government." *Social Science Quarterly* 87(4):882–902.

Green, Jane, and Will Jennings. 2017. *The Politics of Competence: Parties, Public Opinion and Voters*. New York: Cambridge University Press.

Hardin, Russell. 2002. *Trust and Trustworthiness*. New York: Russell Sage Foundation.

Hetherington, Marc J. 2005. *Why Trust Matters: Declining Political Trust and the Demise of American Liberalism*. Princeton, NJ: Princeton University Press.

Hetherington, Marc J., and J. D. Nugent. 2001. "Explaining public support for devolution: The role of political trust." *In What Is It about Government that Americans Dislike*, ed. John R. Hibbing and Elizabeth Theiss-Morse pp. 134–151. Cambridge: Cambridge University Press.

Keele, Luke. 2005. "The authorities really do matter: Party control and trust in government." *Journal of Politics* 67(3):873–886.

Kettl, Donald F. 2019. "From policy to practice: From ideas to results, from results to trust." *Public Administration Review* 79(5): 763–767.

Levi, Margaret. 1998. "A state of trust." *Trust and Governance* 1:77–101.

Listhaug, Ola, and Tor Georg Jakobsen. 2017. "Foundations of political trust." In *The Oxford Handbook of Social and Political Trust*, ed. Eric M. Uslaner, pp. 559–578. New York: Oxford University Press.

March, James G., and Johan P. Olsen. 1989. "Rediscovering institutions: The organizational basis of politics." http://library.wur.nl/WebQuery/clc/1861824.

Miller, Arthur H. 1974. "Political issues and trust in government: 1964–1970." *American Political Science Review* 68(3):951–972.

Newton, Kenneth, Dietlind Stolle, and Sonja Zmerli. 2018. "Social and political trust." In *The Oxford Handbook of Social and Political Trust*, pp. 961–976. New York: Oxford University Press.

Norris, Pippa. 2001. *Digital Divide: Civic Engagement, Information Poverty, and the Internet Worldwide*. Cambridge: Cambridge University Press.

Putnam, Robert D. 1993. *Making Democracy Work*. Princeton, NJ: Princeton University Press.

Putnam, Robert D. 2001. *Bowling Alone: The Collapse and Revival of American Community*. New York: Simon and Schuster.

Rainie, Lee, Scott Keeter, and Andrew Perrin. 2019. "Trust and distrust in America." www.pewresearch.org/politics/2019/10/01/public-expresses-favorable-views-of-a-number-of-federal-agencies/.

Roberts, Alasdair. 2020. "Who should we count as citizens? Categorizing people in public administration research." *Public Administration Review* 81(2):286–290.

Robinson, Scott E., James W. Stoutenborough, and Arnold Vedlitz. 2017. *Understanding Trust in Government: Environmental Sustainability, Fracking, and Public Opinion in American Politics*. Milton Park, UK: Taylor & Francis.

Robinson, Scott E., Joseph T. Ripberger, Kuhika Gupta, Jennis A. Ross, Andrew S. Fox, Hank C. Jenkins Smith, and Carol L. Silva. 2020. "The relevance and operations of political trust in the COVID-19 Pandemic." *Public Administration Review*. https://doi.org/10.1111/puar.13333.

Scholz, John T., and Mark Lubell. 1998. "Trust and taxpaying: Testing the heuristic approach to collective action." *American Journal of Political Science* 398–417.

Siegrist, Michael, George Cvetkovich, and Laudia Roth. 2000. "Salient value similarity, social trust, and risk/benefit perception." *Risk Analysis* 20(3):353–362.

Uslaner, Eric M. 2002. *The Moral Foundations of Trust*. New York: Cambridge University Press.

Uslaner, Eric M. 2018. *The Oxford Handbook of Social and Political Trust*. Oxford: Oxford University Press.

Wolak, Jennifer. 2020. "Why do people trust their state government?" *State Politics & Policy Quarterly* 20(3):313–329.

Wolak, Jennifer, and Christine Kelleher Palus. 2010. "The dynamics of public confidence in US state and local government." *State Politics & Policy Quarterly* 10(4):421–445.

Acknowledgements

This material is based upon work supported by the National Science Foundation under grant no. RAPID-2026763. The authors would also like to thank the offices of the Senior Vice President and Provost and the Vice President for Research and Partnerships for their financial support. This support allowed us to make this volume available as Open Access permanently so that as many people as possible have access to the volume.

Cambridge Elements ⹀

Public and Nonprofit Administration

Andrew Whitford
University of Georgia

Andrew Whitford is Alexander M. Crenshaw Professor of Public Policy in the School of Public and International Affairs at the University of Georgia. His research centers on strategy and innovation in public policy and organization studies.

Robert Christensen
Brigham Young University

Robert Christensen is a professor and George Romney Research Fellow in the Marriott School at Brigham Young University. His research focuses on prosocial and antisocial behaviors and attitudes in public and nonprofit organizations.

About the Series

The foundation of this series are cutting-edge contributions on emerging topics and definitive reviews of keystone topics in public and nonprofit administration, especially those that lack longer treatment in textbook or other formats. Among keystone topics of interest for scholars and practitioners of public and nonprofit administration, it covers public management, public budgeting and finance, nonprofit studies, and the interstitial space between the public and nonprofit sectors, along with theoretical and methodological contributions, including quantitative, qualitative, and mixed-methods pieces.

The Public Management Research Association

The Public Management Research Association improves public governance by advancing research on public organizations, strengthening links among interdisciplinary scholars, and furthering professional and academic opportunities in public management.

Cambridge Elements $\equiv$

Public and Nonprofit Administration

Printed in the United States
by Baker & Taylor Publisher Services